Ernest Hemingway

Titles in the series *Critical Lives* present the work of leading cultural figures of the modern period. Each book explores the life of the artist, writer, philosopher or architect in question and relates it to their major works.

In the same series

Ernest Hemingway

Verna Kale

REAKTION BOOKS

For Michael Dewey DuBose
1983–2014

Published by
REAKTION BOOKS LTD
Unit 32, Waterside
44–48 Wharf Road
London N1 7UX, UK

www.reaktionbooks.co.uk

First published 2016
Copyright © Verna Kale 2016

Printed and bound in Great Britain by Bell & Bain, Glasgow

A catalogue record for this book is available from the British Library

ISBN 978 1 78023 578 3

Contents

Note on the Text

In his personal correspondence, as well as manuscripts and other archival ephemera, Ernest Hemingway frequently misspelled or mistyped words. Sometimes he was in a rush to dash off a letter; other times disability or a faulty typewriter prevented him from making corrections. These errors and unconventional spellings, as well as those by his correspondents or editors, have been retained in the quotations used in this book.

Ernest Hemingway, *c.* 1940.

Prologue

> That was what you did. You died. You did not know what it was about.
> You never had time to learn. They threw you in and told you the rules
> and the first time they caught you off base they killed you.

This passage from the final pages of Ernest Hemingway's novel of
1929, *A Farewell to Arms*, was not the first time the author used the
metaphor of life as a fixed contest, nor would it be the last. 'You
never got away with anything', the novel's protagonist, Frederic
Henry, thinks as his beloved Catherine begs for anaesthesia during
the long and difficult labour that eventually kills her.[1] No one asks
to play the game, everyone plays and everyone loses.

Hemingway's fiction is populated with injured characters
and injured relationships set against a backdrop of the unfeeling
natural world, and there are few, if any, winners. You might, like
Francis Macomber, live a 'short, happy life', but death will find
you: quickly, if you are lucky like Francis, in the form of a crack shot
delivered by your wife; or, if you are not so lucky, slowly, such as
the gangrene infection that leaves the protagonist in 'The Snows
of Kilimanjaro' plenty of time to think about his failed relationships
and unwritten stories on his way out.

In the short story collection *Winner Take Nothing*, of 1933,
the volume's enigmatic epigraph – ghostwritten by Hemingway
himself – instructs the reader, 'the conditions are that the winner
shall take nothing; neither his ease, nor his pleasure, nor any

notions of glory; nor, if he win far enough, shall there be any reward within himself.' Hemingway attested that no matter how well you played the game – or rather, *especially* if you played well – you would end up with nothing in the end. 'It was all a nothing and a man was nothing too . . . he knew it all was *nada y pues nada y nada y pues nada*', he writes in 'A Clean, Well-Lighted Place', one of the anchors of *Winner Take Nothing* and a personal favourite of Hemingway's in the canon of his own work.[2]

Hemingway would live a life fraught with injury and broken relationships, but it was also a life of physical and literary triumph, of intense friendships and love affairs, and it was set against some of the grandest and wildest landscapes in the world. As a war veteran and war correspondent, a hunter and fisherman, an aficionado of the bullfight and an icon of a masculine ideal that he helped shape, Hemingway remained keenly aware that the only way out of the game was death and that the best work of men and women meant nothing in the end.

Hemingway himself proved difficult to kill: he survived mortar attacks and artillery fire, car crashes and plane crashes, dysentery and diabetes, and a host of other illnesses and accidents. In the end, only Hemingway could kill Hemingway, and death came violently to him by his own hand in the early morning hours of 2 July 1961. Yet death was not the end of Ernest Hemingway. His celebrity endures, his books remain in print, and new work from his extensive archive continues to emerge. His own most ambitious work, an interconnected group of manuscripts that explores family, love, sex, death and writing, went unpublished during his lifetime (and much of it remains unpublished still). Meanwhile, his influence on American letters lives on in the work of the writers who succeeded him. He had anticipated no less: as one generation passes, another comes, and all the rivers run into the sea.

1

The Doctor and the Doctor's Wife, 1899–1919

Less than six months shy of the twentieth century, Ernest Miller Hemingway was born into a world of Victorian values, Protestant ethics and middle-class comforts. His father, Clarence Edmonds Hemingway, was a general practice doctor, and his mother, Grace Hall Hemingway, was a trained opera singer, who gave music lessons out of their home. The couple lived with Grace's widowed father, Ernest Hall, in Oak Park, Illinois, an affluent Chicago suburb. The couple had been married in 1896, and had previously welcomed a daughter, Marcelline, in January 1898. Four more siblings – Ursula, Madelaine (nicknamed Sunny), Carol and Leicester – would follow after Ernest, and were born either at home in Oak Park or at the family's summer cabin, Windemere, on Walloon Lake near Petoskey, Michigan.

Young Ernie had a generally happy childhood in which he was encouraged to follow creative pursuits and to develop his skills as an outdoorsman. This upbringing instilled in him a sense of confidence and accomplishment and set him on a trajectory for success that exceeded and, in some ways, exploded his parents' best hopes for him.

From an early age, Hemingway was encouraged by his mother to develop his literary and artistic abilities. Grace notes in the scrapbook she kept for him that he could recite lines from Tennyson and Longfellow and that even as a toddler, he had a gift for metaphor – declaring that a bruise resembled an owl's eye and that a scab looked like a rosebud.[1]

Ernest Hemingway, fishing with his sister Marcelline in Walloon Lake near Petoskey, Michigan, in July 1901.

From his father, Hemingway inherited a love of the outdoors and an affinity for hunting and fishing. For Ernie's third birthday, he went on a fishing trip with his father and caught his first fish, landing it by himself, and he loved playing outdoors at Windemere. Hemingway's interest in the wilderness reflects a certain spirit of the age, as it was at this time that the nascent environmentalist movement began to take hold in America. Hemingway was born in the same decade that saw the founding of the Sierra Club and the establishment of Yosemite National Park. In 1904, the same year that Hemingway joined his father's chapter of the Agassiz Club, his boyhood hero, President Theodore Roosevelt, was elected to a second term. Under Roosevelt, 125 million acres were added to the national forests, 51 bird sanctuaries were established and eighteen natural wonders came under federal protection.[2] In keeping with contemporary ideas of conservation, the boys in the Agassiz Club collected specimens, killing them as needed, bottling them or pinning them to cards, identifying them and putting them on display. When Hemingway went east with his mother for a visit to the Massachusetts island of Nantucket, he wrote home to his father asking if he ought to take advantage of an opportunity to buy an albatross foot for the club's collections.[3]

Hemingway inherited some of his parents' less desirable traits as well: poor eyesight from his mother and from his father, a susceptibility to type 2 diabetes. Clarence and Grace likely passed on some mental health issues, such as bipolar disorder and depression, though of course problems like these were not discussed openly in the polite society to which the family belonged. Clarence's dark mood swings were bad enough that he likely sought out treatment under the guise of attending courses in medical training.[4] His depression, in addition to his angina, diabetes and despondency over unwise investments, eventually drove Clarence to take his own life in 1928, an act that left a permanent mark on Ernest's psyche. In his personal correspondence, Hemingway writes of the possibility of his own suicide so often that, even as a young man, he seems to have considered it an inevitability, at worst, and at best a way of extorting sympathy from his correspondents.

Hemingway with toy pistol, his sisters Madelaine, Ursula and Marcelline, paternal grandfather Anson Hemingway in his Civil War uniform, and cousins Margaret and Virginia Hemingway on Decoration Day, 1907.

Hemingway's relationship with his parents has often been portrayed as an acrimonious one, but the family dynamic was more complicated than that. The bipolar disorder that likely affected both the parents and the son is mirrored in his relationship with them. Hemingway sought, and won, their love and approval and thanked them dutifully in letters home for their financial support and concern for his well-being.

Though he was noticeably influenced by both parents, the young Hemingway also regularly challenged their conservative beliefs and practices, and frequently got himself into trouble. Most of his exploits were innocent enough, though traces of his adult adventures to come – hunting, boxing and subverting convention – are visible in these childhood scrapes. His mother's scrapbooks reveal that Hemingway acted out in church and in school, and he got in trouble for gratuitously killing a porcupine, shooting a blue heron, running from the game warden and using his mother's music room as a boxing ring.[5] Hemingway's pious parents – they were Congregationalists – required that their children confess and repent any wrongdoing. His mother pasted one such 'Confession' into Ernie's scrapbook: 'My conduct at the [missionary exposition] yesterday was bad and my conduct this morning in church was bad my conduct tomorrow will be good.'[6]

Hemingway later assigned great significance to the shooting of the blue heron, a protected species, writing about the incident in the 1950s in 'The Last Good Country'. In this fragment of an unfinished novel, Hemingway's avatar Nick Adams and his little sister run away from home to escape two game wardens who want to prosecute Nick for illegal hunting and for selling trout. The siblings disappear into the Michigan wilderness, crossing into virgin timber that few others have ever seen. The scene makes Nick feel 'strange. Like the way [he] ought to feel in church.'[7]

Like his protagonists, Hemingway had a complicated relationship with organized religion, struggling with the piety of his parents yet finding himself drawn to the traditions of Catholicism, but he consistently found solace, even redemption, in nature.[8] 'The Last Good Country' is not the only time that Nick Adams would seek healing in the countryside; in 'Big Two-Hearted River' (1925), an older Nick retreats into the Michigan landscape to escape the unspoken traumas of the First World War. The self-sufficiency of making one's own way, carrying one's own gear and cooking one's own food allows the protagonist to heal from the wounds of civilization: war, game laws and even the petty arguments among family members. 'Haven't we seen enough fights in families?' Nick's sister asks him in 'The Last Good Country'.[9]

Even when outwardly contrite, Hemingway's sense of humour (and an early affinity for literary allusion) is visible in his account of his father's discovery of the music room pugilism: 'Did dad break-up that little social tea? Wow . . . Dad certainly rose to the occassion in the oratory line. Demosthenes, – Cicero, Daniel Webster – didn't have anything on my worthy pater. Anyway boxing is now frouned upon in this household.'[10] Other altercations with the family did not blow over so easily. The summer that Hemingway turned 21, he helped his younger siblings and their friends sneak out for a late-night picnic on Walloon Lake. Angry at what she saw as further evidence of her now-grown son's irresponsibility, Grace ordered him to leave Windemere and, in an extended metaphor comparing a mother's love to a bank account, accused him of overdrawing the funds of her affection. She admonished him: 'Do not come back until your tongue has learned not to insult and shame your mother.'[11]

Though Grace told Hemingway she would be 'waiting to welcome [him]' and 'longing' for his love, Hemingway – who was, by this time, already a decorated veteran of the American Red Cross ambulance service – felt as if he had been disowned.[12] It may have felt like rejection to Hemingway, but Grace and Clarence appear to have been more concerned than angry and determined to practise tough love with their eldest son, who they hoped would go to university or find regular work. Clarence wrote to Grace that he was continually praying that Ernest 'will develop a sense of greater responsibility' and that he 'must get busy and make his own way'.[13] His parents were determined not to give in to their son, and instead to allow him to suffer the consequences of what they felt was an idle lifestyle in danger of damaging his immortal soul.

Though Ernest's relationship with Grace would remain tumultuous, after she was widowed in 1928 the author took care of her with literal bank deposits, establishing a trust fund with profits from *A Farewell to Arms* and supporting her financially until her death in 1951. Nevertheless, the incident at Windemere marks the last summer Hemingway would spend there with the family. Though he would return at least twice more for short visits, he never again spent another summer on the lake.

There were strains elsewhere in the Hemingway household as well. In a letter to his mother from 1917, Ernest asks her not to 'burn any papers in [his] room or throw away anything that you don't like the looks of'.[14] The precedent Hemingway has for this concern is unknown, although a fictionalized version of such a scene occurs in the short story 'Now I Lay Me', published in *Men Without Women* (1927), in which Nick's mother burns his father's collection of artefacts and scientific specimens. In the story, Nick, convalescing in an Italian hospital and afraid he will die in his sleep, keeps himself awake at night by systematically remembering his past. Nick remembers specimen jars burning in a bonfire in the yard; presumably they belonged to his father and were burned by his mother, though Nick claims he 'could not remember who burned the things'. He recalls, too, that his 'mother was always cleaning things out and making a good clearance'.[15] When his father comes home to find the collection of Indian artefacts burning in the yard, he commands Nick to get a rake, but the best arrowheads are already ruined. The incident, should it have occurred in

Hemingway's own life, would have taken place following the family's move to their new house in 1906, making Hemingway only six years old, but the letter home in 1917 suggests that Grace, like Nick's mother, was likely to have purged her home of unwanted objects, a move that would have asserted her dominance over the household and belittled the scientific interests of her husband.

Later in life, Hemingway referred to Grace as an 'all American bitch', and characters such as the passive-aggressive titular matriarch in 'The Doctor and the Doctor's Wife' (1924) or the emotionally blackmailing Mrs Krebs in 'Soldier's Home' (1925) are commonly viewed as fictionalized portraits of her.[16] The reality of the mother–son relationship, however, is more fraught, and whatever he may have said in his correspondence with others or in fiction, Hemingway's letters to Grace herself reveal a dutiful son as eager to win his mother's approval as he was to impress the literary critics.

His adolescence brought with it the usual challenges to parental authority and the daily routines typical of suburban life. Hemingway participated in a range of extracurricular activities and, as he got older, cultivated an active social life, mainly 'bumming' with friends, but also occasionally taking girls on dates – and then enduring the teasing of his friends and siblings for it. In high school, Hemingway began publishing short stories in the school literary magazine, *The Tabula*. Featuring boxers, hunters and Indians, these pieces of juvenilia contain a similar cast of characters to his mature stories, but where Hemingway's later work would often leave its central conflict unstated, trusting the reader to understand nuances the text only implied, these early works rely on blood-soaked melodrama to move the plot towards the kind of 'twist' endings commonly found in the popular fiction of the day. Nevertheless, the young Hemingway likely sensed that his work had an edginess not right for the conservative mass market publications to which his family subscribed. In 'The Last Good Country', the young would-be author Nick proclaims his stories 'too morbid for the *St Nicholas*', a national monthly magazine for youth that published work by established writers as well as reader submissions.[17] Hemingway need not have worried about the conservative tastes of a U.S. readership because, in just a few years, his work would be welcomed in the little magazines of expatriate Paris.

Hemingway also worked on the school newspaper, *The Trapeze*, and after his high school graduation, when his sister Marcelline and many of his friends went off to university, he applied for a job at the *Kansas City Star*. In the autumn of 1917 he headed to Kansas City to begin his apprenticeship as a newspaperman.[18]

Staying, at first, in the home of his uncle Tyler Hemingway, who had helped him find the job, but soon getting an apartment with Carl Edgar, a friend from his Michigan summers, Hemingway began working as a cub reporter at the *Star*. He worked the hospital beat and covered the 19th Street police station.[19] Hemingway was excited to have the use of a desk and a typewriter at his disposal in the newsroom, as well as access to work space in the Muehlebach Hotel, and he was proud to be working for a 'pretty influential' paper with a circulation of 200,000.[20]

Though Kansas City would barely figure in his later fiction, the six-and-a-half months that Hemingway spent at the *Star* nevertheless had a lasting impact on the writer's developing style. It was at the *Star* that Hemingway received what he later deemed 'the best rules I ever learned for the business of writing'.[21] The *Star* copy style sheet instructs writers to 'Use short sentences. Use short first paragraphs. Use vigorous English' and 'Eliminate every superfluous word.'[22] These qualities would become hallmarks of Hemingway's much-imitated style.

Hemingway's pieces at the *Star* were uncredited and likely bore the influence of the desk editor, rewrite men and copy-editors, but, based on descriptions of the stories Hemingway said he covered, a number of articles have been attributed to him with some certainty. With a hard-boiled cast of characters – a prizefighter not quite 1.5 metres (5 ft) tall, feuding drug dealers and government agents, and a typesetter distraught at what the amputation of his thumb will mean for his craft – the dialogue-heavy accounts prefigure such fictional inventions as Ole Anderson, Harry Morgan, Richard Cantwell and other 'bullfighters, bruisers, touts, gunmen, professional soldiers, prostitutes, hard-drinkers, dope-fiends' and their 'sordid little catastrophes'.[23] The stories possess a certain artistry that goes beyond reporting the news from the general hospital. Hemingway brings readers into the scene as the ambulance 'speeds down the Cherry Street hill, the headlights boring a yellow funnel into the darkness'.[24]

His letters home are exuberant with accounts of his adventures, and he boasts to Marcelline, 'I can tell Mayors to go to Hell and slap Police commissioners on the Back! Yeah tis indeed the existence.'[25] He also claimed that the work was dangerous enough that he had to carry a handgun.[26] In a letter to his father, he describes the hectic pace of the newsroom:

> Having to write a half column story with every name, address and initial verified and remembering to use good style, perfect style in fact, an get all the facts and in the correct order, make it have snap and wallop and write it in fifteen minutes, five sentences at a time to catch an edition as it goes to press. To take a story over the phone and get evrything exact see it all in your minds eye, rush over to a typewriter and write it a page at a time while ten other typewriters are going and the boss is hollering at some one and a boy snatches the pages from your machine as fast as you write them.[27]

As the war in Europe escalated, Hemingway wrote items for the *Star* about local recruitment efforts and men seeking 'action and danger'.[28] Hemingway craved adventure, and, though he was delighted with his newfound independence and the excitement of reporting, he was also eager to take part in the fighting in Europe. When Austria-Hungary invaded Serbia in July 1914, Hemingway was about to start his sophomore year of high school, but the First World War waited for him. The U.S. entered the war in April 1917, shortly before Hemingway's high school graduation, and now, after six months at the *Star*, the nineteen-year-old Hemingway was ready to head 'Over There' himself.

Though he talked of enlisting in the Marines with Carl Edgar and Bill Smith, another Michigan friend working in Kansas City, to Hemingway's disappointment – and likely to his parents' relief – he had little chance of being taken into the armed forces thanks to congenital vision loss in his left eye.[29] While he bided his time in Kansas City, he joined the Missouri Home Guard, and he wrote to his family with excitement about the drills and the uniforms.[30] He told Marcelline that he was determined to get over to the war 'not because of any love of gold braid glory etc. but because [he] couldnt face any body after the war and not have been in it'.[31] Nevertheless, Hemingway was hoping for one last summer up in Michigan before departing for Europe.[32] As it turned out, Hemingway would spend most of that summer in Italy.

Hemingway had been at the *Star* about a month when he met Theodore ('Ted') Brumback, who had recently returned from France, where he had served as an ambulance driver in the American Field Service. Brumback joined the newsroom as a cub reporter, and, like Hemingway, failed to qualify for the Armed Forces because of vision problems. Brumback's stories about the fighting in France and the heroics of the ambulance drivers doubtless impressed Hemingway, who was four years Brumback's junior. In February 1918 Brumback published in the paper a long narrative account of his wartime experiences in which he described dodging enemy shells and gas. Familiar with Brumback's story, and perhaps acting on a lead he garnered while interviewing Red Cross recruiters for a news item, Hemingway finally settled on a plan of action and volunteered for the ambulance service in Italy.[33]

In March 1918 he wrote to his sister that he had, in fact, enlisted as a driver and that 'it is a big relief to be enlisted in sometging' but that she should not tell the family yet.[34] Having filled its immediate need, however, the Red Cross did not call Hemingway and Brumback up until the first week of May, but then things moved forwards quickly. The *Star* acknowledged the departure of its two former journalists with a brief item that ran beneath portraits of the men in the edition of the paper on 13 May 1918.[35] They spent two weeks together in New York City with other Red Cross recruits, and on 23 May they set sail for Bordeaux in France.[36]

From Bordeaux the volunteers headed to Paris by train and heard the first booms of German shelling. Another train ride followed, and Hemingway's first assignment in Italy was to collect the dismembered remains of factory workers killed in an explosion at a munitions plant. Hemingway would later recreate that episode in his short story 'A Natural History of the Dead' (1932).[37] It was a horrifying spectacle, but to the young adventurer, it was also thrilling. On 9 June 1918 Hemingway sent cheerful postcards to his father and to friends at the *Star* announcing that he was headed to the front the next day.[38] Finally Hemingway found himself in Schio, a village in the foothills of the Dolomite mountains, only 16 kilometres (10 miles) from the Italian and Austro-Hungarian line.[39] A provisional second lieutenant, Hemingway soon grew bored with the camp-like atmosphere of what the guys called the 'Schio Country Club' and longed to see more action.[40] He got his chance when the Red Cross sought volunteers to staff canteens near Fossalta, by the Piave river, where fighting had intensified.

Hemingway internalized these experiences, and the people and places would appear, reimagined, in his fiction in the years to come: places like the Villa Rossa brothel, where the bored lieutenant Frederic Henry wasted his time in *A Farewell to Arms* before meeting

Catherine Barkley, or the silkworm 'farm' where his friend Bill Horne was stationed and which would make an appearance in the short story 'Now I Lay Me' in 1927. The most significant event of Hemingway's young life, the event that would most heavily influence his early writing, however, was still to come.

In the early hours of 8 July, Hemingway was delivering chocolate, cigarettes and postcards to the troops entrenched on the Piave when an Austrian mortar hit the ground and sent shrapnel flying in every direction. Hemingway describes Frederic Henry's similar wounding in *A Farewell to Arms*:

> I heard a cough, then came the chuh-chuh-chuh-chuh – then there was a flash, as when a blast-furnace door is swung open, and a roar that started white and went red and on and on in a rushing wind. I tried to breathe but my breath would not come and I felt myself rush bodily out of myself and out and out and out and all the time bodily in the wind. I went out swiftly, all of myself, and I knew I was dead and that it had all been a mistake to think you just died. Then I floated, and instead of going on I felt myself slide back. I breathed and I was back. The ground was torn up and in front of my head there was a splintered beam of wood. In the jolt of my head I heard somebody crying.[41]

There is some inconsistency in the accounts of what exactly happened in the moments after the wounding – about whether Hemingway carried a wounded comrade to safety (probably not) and about the exact nature of his injuries (both an official report and Hemingway himself count 227 punctures).[42] The *Kansas City Star* would report that Hemingway was the first casualty among the former *Star* employees in service; indeed, Hemingway is reportedly the first surviving American casualty on the Italian front (another American in the canteen service had been killed the previous month).[43] Hemingway was taken to a field hospital before being transferred to Milan. All in all, less than two months had elapsed between Hemingway's departure from New York and his transport to Milan, where he would spend the next six months recuperating.

Brumback, visiting Hemingway in the hospital in Milan, wrote to the Hemingway family because Hemingway had shrapnel in his fingers and was unable to wield a pen. Brumback reassured them that Ernest was receiving 'the best care in Europe' and speculated that by the time the letter arrived, Hemingway would be back in his section.[44] Hemingway was soon well enough to write to his parents himself and reported he had picked up as many 'souveniers' as he could carry from among the dead Austrians so numerous 'the ground was almost black with them' and that he had 'glimpsed the making of large gobs of history'.[45] Despite his high spirits, Hemingway had months of recuperation ahead of him, and his legs remained in splints as he awaited an operation to remove the embedded pieces of metal.[46]

He wrote home asking his parents to send him local papers and the *Saturday Evening Post* and begged his sisters to write to him (and to encourage friends to write to him).[47] In late September he went on convalescent leave in Stresa, on the shore of Lake Maggiore in Italy. He continued to store away his experiences for later use: Frederic Henry and Catherine Barkley would row across this lake during their escape into neutral Switzerland, and Count Greffi, a minor character in the novel, is based upon Count Giuseppe Greppi, the 'Old Count Grecco', whom Hemingway befriended at his hotel. Hemingway described him in a letter home: nearly 100 years old and 'perfectly preserved', the Count 'never married, goes to bed at midnight and smokes and drinks champagne' – to Hemingway's nineteen-year-old eyes, the Count represented a masculine ideal.[48]

Yet permanent bachelorhood was not an ideal to which Hemingway himself aspired – he was in love with an American nurse, the 26-year-old Agnes von Kurowsky, with whom he had shared late-night chats, chaperoned dates, stolen kisses and perhaps

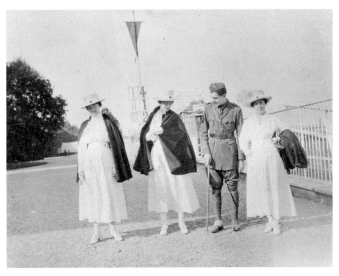

Ernest Hemingway, in his Italian uniform, at a racetrack in Milan with Red Cross nurses. Agnes von Kurowsky is second from left.

more. It was no schoolboy crush, he assured Marcelline – Agnes was the girl he would 'really love always'. He confided in Marcelline that though he was in no position to marry Agnes now, he planned to marry her in two years. This waiting period was likely Agnes's decree rather than his own, for Hemingway was already referring to her as 'the wife'.[49]

Agnes, meanwhile, had left for Treviso to care for victims of the influenza outbreak that had begun earlier that year.[50] The death toll of the flu pandemic was staggering – up to 10 per cent of the world's population between the ages of 20 and 30 died of the disease, and it had a worldwide death toll of 50 to 100 million – but Hemingway, who wrote to his father that 'it has been fairly conclusively proved that I cant be bumped off', was eager to get back into action.[51] He joined his colleagues in the ambulance service near Bassano but was almost immediately taken ill with jaundice and compelled to return to the hospital.[52] The Vittorio-Veneto campaign proved to be the last major battle in Italy, and on 3 November Austria-Hungary entered into an armistice agreement with Italy; Germany's armistice with the Allies followed soon after on 11 November, ending the fighting in Europe.[53] Hemingway was almost fully recovered, and the war was over.

With Agnes nudging him to go stateside with vague promises of marriage, Hemingway decided that it was time to return home. 'I am going to commence the real war again', he wrote to his family, 'The war to make the world Safe for Ernie Hemingway and I plan to knock 'em for a loop and will be a busy man for several years.'[54] How he planned to go about the task was clear: 'I was made to be one of those beastly writing chaps y'Know.'[55] Full of optimism about the future, Hemingway set sail for the u.s. on 4 January 1919.

2

The Age Demanded, 1919–22

Hemingway returned home to a town that was populated by '80,000,000,000,000 males – mostly fat and exempt crying out for second hand thrills to be got from the front'.[1] Ostensibly reluctant to play the role of the returned hero – 'the real heroes are dead', he wrote to his friend Jim Gamble – Hemingway nevertheless cut quite a figure walking around town in his Italian uniform, which included a cape. He carried a cane and walked with a limp and entertained school children with tales of war.[2]

Twice the Hemingway home was overtaken by local Italian-Americans, celebrating their recently returned honorary countryman, and red wine flowed in great abundance in the otherwise teetotal household.[3] Nevertheless, Hemingway found Oak Park dull, he missed Agnes, and he felt disconnected from the life he had known for the past two and a half years. 'I'm patriotic and willing to die for this great and glorious nation,' he wrote to Gamble, 'But I hate like the deuce to live in it.'[4] He kept himself busy writing stories and told Gamble he planned to inundate the *Saturday Evening Post* with submissions. He was full of enthusiasm, blissfully unaware that the *Post* would not accept any of his work – then or ever.

What had been a manageable state of ennui, however, turned to devastation when he received a letter from Agnes informing him of her engagement to someone else. Her earlier letters had contained hints of her shifting affections, but Hemingway was 'just smashed' by the break-up nonetheless.[5] The age difference, which had not seemed to bother Hemingway in the least, did concern Agnes, who wrote 'I am still very fond of you, but, it is more as a mother than as a sweetheart . . . I am now & always will be too old, & that's the truth, & I can't get away from the fact that you're just a boy – a kid.'[6] Agnes's letter was forthright but not cruel, and she clearly recognized in him a latent talent: 'some day I'll have reason to be proud of you', she wrote, and she expressed hope that he would be able to forgive her and 'start a wonderful career'.[7]

Agnes was, of course, right: Hemingway would have a wonderful career. However, she could hardly have predicted the extent to which she would influence his writing. Most obviously, Agnes's presence is felt in the pages of *A Farewell to Arms*, but before Hemingway gave the world the resolute Catherine Barkley, he reimagined her as Ag in Chapter Ten of *in our time* (1924) (republished in 1925 as 'A Very Short Story' in *In Our Time*). Like Agnes and Catherine Barkley, Ag – or 'Luz', as she is called in later editions – works as the night nurse in the Italian hospital where the American protagonist lies wounded.[8] Also like Agnes and Catherine, Ag preps her young soldier-beau for surgery by administering an enema. And, like Agnes and Hemingway, Ag and the soldier have an argument on a train from Padua to Milan about her hesitation to return stateside with him.[9] The penultimate paragraph of the story is a faithful paraphrase of Agnes's break-up letter to him, right down to the wishes for a 'great career'.[10]

With its candid sexual content, the story leaves readers wondering about Agnes and Hemingway. Henry Villard, a veteran who knew both parties, insists that Agnes never went to bed with Hemingway.[11] Nevertheless, 'A Very Short Story' eroticizes the nurse–patient relationship. The nurse's preparation of the patient for surgery is depicted as a form of play, and nurse and patient switch roles: she lies in the (post-coital) bed as the soldier limps around the ward, doing her rounds.

Agnes has largely been read as a free spirit who resisted Hemingway's attempts to pin her down, even advising Hemingway not to write to her so frequently, as she hadn't the time to read his letters, but there may have been more to the break-up than the satisfaction of her own whims.[12] With the selflessness of those for whom the nursing profession is a calling as much as it is a career, Agnes may have been looking out for the bright young man's best interests. Decades later she stated in an interview that she broke up with Hemingway in part to preserve the integrity of his future career. Convincing him to move back home to wait for her – and then dumping him – was her way of protecting the impressionable young man from taking up with a wealthy friend who had offered to finance a year-long jaunt around Europe.[13] In her telling of the events, she got him out of harm's way by settling him back home in the States rather than allowing him to embark on precisely the kind of life of dissipation that would later trouble the characters of *The Sun Also Rises* (1926). In that novel, Jake's friend Bill teases him:

> You're an expatriate. You've lost touch with the soil. You get precious. Fake European standards have ruined you. You drink yourself to death. You become obsessed by sex. You spend all your time talking, not working. You are an expatriate, see? You hang around cafés.[14]

Though Hemingway claimed to friends to have 'cauterize[d]' the wound Agnes left in his heart 'with a course of booze and other women', the injury was not so easily cured, and the love affair not so easily forgotten.[15] He wrote to Agnes in 1922 – when he was newly married – and she responded with a letter congratulating him on his recent marriage and recounting her nursing adventures in Russia, Eastern Europe and New York. Her tone was friendly and, though wistful, revealed no regret about any missed opportunities, except those related to her career.[16] Nothing came of the brief exchange, though he would fictionalize it as yet another missed opportunity in 'The Snows of Kilimanjaro' (1936): dying on the African plains, a writer who has given himself over to the material comforts offered by his wealthy companion – a woman who, with her disposable, inherited wealth, bears some resemblance to Hemingway's second wife – recalls 'the first one, the one who left him'.[17] The dying writer remembers how he had written a letter to his first love, confessing his longing for her, and how later, after he had forgotten all about the letter, she wrote back, only for the letter to be intercepted by his wife. There would be no reconciliation – either in the fiction or in real life.

In 1922, the year that Hemingway reconnected with Agnes – and also the approximate year in the fictional world of 'Snows' that the protagonist, witness to events of the Graeco-Turkish war, writes to his first love – the memories of her would still have been fresh. This was also the year that Hemingway was back on European soil for the first time since the war, so his attempt to make contact makes sense. But archival evidence also suggests that in 1957, four decades removed from his relationship with Agnes, Hemingway again sought out information on her whereabouts.[18] The Red Cross responded with the information that Agnes, now married, was living in Key West – just 160 kilometres (100 miles) away from Hemingway's home in Cuba. It is not difficult to imagine the ageing Hemingway, a public figure, caught up in the many responsibilities of domestic life and struggling to complete any one of the unfinished manuscripts in his possession, daydreaming about a simpler time when he was not yet famous and wondering what had happened to the woman he first loved. Though it would have been simple for Hemingway to visit Agnes in Key West from his home outside Havana, and she herself knew of his whereabouts, she did not seek him out on any of her occasional trips to Cuba, and they never met again in person.[19]

Within weeks of the break-up, however, Hemingway was writing to friends claiming the end of the affair was for the best: 'I'm now free to do whatever I want. Go whereever I want and have all the time in the world to develop into some kind of a writer.'[20] However, Hemingway was no Harold Krebs, the protagonist of Hemingway's short story 'Soldier's Home' (1925). Though the strained relationships in the Krebs family are often read as reflections of tensions in the Hemingway household, there are a number of key biographical differences between Krebs and Hemingway.[21] Krebs had been a university student and fraternity brother before he joined the American Expeditionary Force, while Hemingway had decided against university. Krebs saw combat in some of the more gruesome engagements of the First World War, whereas Hemingway's wounding while distributing chocolates shares much more in common with that of Frederic Henry in *A Farewell to Arms*, who was 'blown up while . . . eating cheese'.[22]

Hemingway, like Krebs, had a loving relationship with his little sister, but, unlike Krebs, his relationship with his parents was also generally good – or it at least exhibited only the same conflicts any young man who has been abroad and developed a taste for grappa and adventure might have with his more conservative parents upon returning home. Getting out of the house but not straying too far, Hemingway spent the summer and autumn in Michigan, fishing, visiting friends and working on his fiction. He wrote to his parents often. The Hemingways were again urging their son to go to university, but the interactions bore little in common with the emotional blackmail enacted by Krebs's mother as she begs Harold to pray with her and to admit that he loves his 'Mummy'.[23]

At the end of 'Soldier's Home', Krebs decides he will head to Kansas City to get a job. Hemingway, however, would not be heading back to Missouri. Instead, he got an offer from Ralph and Harriet Connable, a wealthy couple with Petoskey ties who were now based in Toronto, to take a paid position as a companion to their disabled son Ralph Jr, while the family went on an extended vacation in Palm Beach. In January 1920 Hemingway, ready for a change of scenery and in need of a job, moved to Toronto.[24] He wasn't crazy about the location – 'just like evry other damn city, a milling, stinking, sweating money grubbing place' – but the duties of his position in the Connable household were light, and he soon took on freelance work writing features for the *Star Weekly*, the Sunday magazine published by the Toronto *Daily Star*.[25]

Torn between several possibilities – returning to Italy, working on a steamship or seeking work in Kansas City or New York – Hemingway once again displayed the lack of focus that so concerned his parents.[26] In October 1920 Hemingway accepted an invitation to Chicago. There he initially took up residence with Y. K. Smith, brother of Hemingway's friends Bill and Katy Smith, and Smith's wife. He was soon bringing in some money freelancing for the *Toronto Star Weekly*, moved into his own apartment with his friend Bill Horne and, failing to break into the advertising business, in December found a steady paycheck writing for *The Cooperative Commonwealth*, the mouthpiece of the Cooperative Society of America. Hemingway's confidence in the unscrupulous organization seems dubious – even when boasting of his new job to his mother, he wrote, cagily, 'If almost any part of what they say about this movement is true it is quelque movement', and he estimates that most of the magazine was written by him. In an offhand statement that both excuses this shady work and foreshadows an important aspect of his longer career, he professes, 'Will write anything once.'[27]

Far more important to his career than the hack work he did for *The Cooperative Commonwealth* were the connections he made in Chicago – connections that would eventually give him the inspiration and means with which to break out of familiar surroundings and to get over to Paris, where he would finally be able to develop his considerable, if raw, talent. It was in Chicago that he first met Sherwood Anderson, whose collection of short stories,

Winesburg, Ohio (1919), had garnered much critical success: in a review from 1919 published in the *Chicago American*, the prominent critic H. L. Mencken called it 'some of the most remarkable writing done in America in our time'.[28] That Mencken uses a phrase that would later serve as the title of two of Hemingway's earliest books is coincidental but nevertheless telling, reflecting Anderson's place in a literary movement obsessed with its own modernity. As vociferously as Hemingway would later deny it, Anderson would deeply influence Hemingway's earliest work, and his mentorship played a key role in establishing Hemingway as an up-and-coming author at a time when he had little published writing on which to trade.

Hemingway made another important connection in Chicago when Katy Smith introduced Hadley Richardson, her old school friend, to the group. Twenty-eight-year-old Hadley, originally from St Louis, caught Hemingway's attention with her skilled piano playing and lovely red hair, and by December he was professing his love for her: 'my loving you is a chink in the armour of telling the world to go to hell and you can thrust a sword into it at any time.'[29] The relationship quickly grew even more serious as they discussed a shared future, and Hadley was willing to follow Hemingway to Europe and to support his writing career with her trust fund. For his 22nd birthday, she gave him a Corona typewriter, another indication of her faith in his talent. Hadley, whose parents were both deceased, was eager to escape her native St Louis, where she had led a somewhat sheltered life with an overbearing older sister, and she felt little compulsion to hold the wedding in her hometown.[30] The couple were married on 3 September 1921, at the Methodist Church in Horton Bay, Michigan, and rowed across Walloon Lake to honeymoon at Windemere.[31] Summers there had provided a backdrop for a number of flirtations prior to his relationship with Hadley, including a possible liaison with Prudence Boulton, a Native American teenager whom Hemingway later writes

Ernest Hemingway and Hadley Richardson on their wedding day, 3 September 1921, in Horton Bay, Michigan, with Hemingway's sisters Carol and Ursula, mother Grace Hall Hemingway, brother Leicester, and father Clarence Edmonds Hemingway.

Signatures of honeymooners Hadley Richardson Hemingway and Ernest Hemingway in the guestbook at Windemere, the family summer home on Walloon Lake near Petoskey, Michigan.

about as 'Trudy' – the girl whom Nick recalls 'did first what no one has ever done better'.[32] Prudence, who committed suicide in 1918, was gone when Hemingway returned to Michigan with his bride, but other girlfriends remained and, to Hadley's embarrassment, Hemingway took his new wife around Petoskey introducing her to his old flames.[33] This move foretells Hemingway's need to have a charming woman at his side and suggests a certain amount of insecurity on his part that, in later years, would be assuaged by his assemblage of other groups of admirers, both male and female.

For the time being, however, Hadley was enough, and the couple enjoyed an intimate relationship that fed off the excitement of their adventures. They set sail for France in December 1921. Hemingway had originally planned to return to Italy, but Anderson urged him that Paris was the place for an aspiring young writer, and the author provided Hemingway with letters of introduction to some of the most important names in the Paris expatriate literary scene, including Gertrude Stein, Ezra Pound and Sylvia Beach. In his letter, Anderson praised his unpublished protégé as 'an American writer instinctively in touch with everything worth while going on here'.[34]

Stein, who had moved to Paris in 1903, was well known, even back home in America, as the doyenne of a salon at 27 rue de Fleurus, and her experiments with 'automatic writing' – the literary application of the scientific experiments on the human subconscious she had conducted at the Harvard Psychological Laboratory in 1896 – attracted both curiosity and derision from American middlebrow readers who didn't know what to make of *Tender Buttons* (1914).[35] Though Stein's stream-of-consciousness poetry, which relied heavily on repetition and word-association, vexed American audiences, Anderson defended the writer's literary importance in the spring 1922 issue of *The Little Review*, writing that she is 'a woman of striking vigour, a subtle and powerful mind, a discrimination in the arts such as I have found in no other American born man or woman and a charmingly brilliant conversationalist',

Portrait of Prudence Boulton, a Native American girl whom Hemingway knew from his Michigan summers and who presumably inspired the characters Prudence Mitchell of 'Ten Indians' and Trudy Gilby of 'Fathers and Sons' and 'The Last Good Country'. Her father was Dick Boulton; a character by that name appears in 'The Doctor and the Doctor's Wife'.

and declaring hers 'the most important pioneer work done in the field of letters in my time'.[36]

Pound, an American expatriate since 1908 whose Paris tenure actually lasted only from 1920 to 1924, helped to shape the literary movement fomenting there during his brief stay. An important poet himself, Pound was also a literary talent scout, funnelling work to Harriet Monroe's *Poetry*, Margaret Anderson's *The Little Review* and Scofield Thayer's *The Dial*. Where Stein would influence Hemingway's nascent stylistic experiments, Pound would serve as an advocate and agent, helping Hemingway to place some of his earliest works in the little magazines and introducing him to other literary personalities around the Latin Quarter.

Then there was Beach, not a writer herself but nevertheless an influential personality who operated the bookstore and lending library Shakespeare and Company at 12 rue de l'Odéon. The shop served as a communications hub of sorts for the expatriates, and it was Beach who in 1922 first published James Joyce's *Ulysses* in its entirety when others would not touch the controversial novel. There Hemingway was able to satisfy his voracious appetite for reading material. He was Beach's 'best customer', a regular who came in to read the magazines and newspapers and who actually 'spent money on books, a trait very pleasing to the proprietor of a small book business'.[37] Hemingway's memories of the place, though equally fond, differ somewhat from Beach's: he would later recall in his posthumously published memoir, *A Moveable Feast* (1964), that 'in those days there was no money to buy books' and confesses that he was 'very shy' when he first entered the bookshop and joined the lending library on credit. 'There was no reason for her to trust me', he claimed, noting that his Paris address above a nightclub at 74 rue Cardinal Lemoine 'could not have been a poorer one'.[38] Beach, on the other hand, recalls a young man with a deep voice who, upon their first meeting, needed little coaxing to take off his shoes and socks to show off his war wounds and who related some tall tales of combat, both in the war and in the boxing ring.[39] Beach recognized that Hemingway's bravado was, to some degree, an act, and she reports that Joyce suggested 'it was a mistake, Hemingway's thinking himself such a tough fellow and [the poet and publisher Robert] McAlmon trying to pass himself off as the sensitive type' when 'it was the other way around'.[40]

In any event, Hemingway was not shy enough to need Anderson's letter, which Hemingway did not get around to giving Beach until after he had already made her acquaintance on his own. At Shakespeare and Company Hemingway made broad use of the lending library, making up for his lack of a college education and absorbing the lessons that Tolstoy and Dostoyevsky had to teach as well as checking out his competition among the other modernists. Hemingway's work evinces a wide range of literary influences – from Robert Louis Stevenson and Rudyard Kipling, to Mark Twain and Stephen Crane, to Sherwood Anderson and Gertrude Stein – but Hemingway was not interested in blindly following existing patterns. Beach notes that, despite his voracious appetite for literary fiction, the person 'who taught him to write . . . was Ernest Hemingway'.[41]

Indeed, Hemingway's tense relationship with his contemporaries – and his precursors – emerges as a theme in *A Moveable Feast* and can be seen from his interactions with his fellow expatriates from his earliest days in Paris, even as he was eager to gain acceptance into their circles. It was partly this need to distance himself from these perceived influences that drove his eventual falling out with Anderson, but when he was still just making his way in his new town, he was happy to follow Anderson's recommendations, not just on who was who, but practical advice on where to stay and dine.

As Anderson had suggested, when they arrived in Paris in late December 1921, the Hemingways took up residence on the Left Bank in the Hotel Jacob. In a letter that tries a bit too hard to be writerly – the rum they drink is 'like the Holy Spirit', the Spanish hillsides they had glimpsed from their boat 'like tired dinosaurs' and the lighthouse is 'like a little candle stuck up on the dinosaurs shoulder' – Hemingway wrote to Anderson, thanking him for his help.[42]

The Hemingways didn't stay long in Paris before heading out on a trip to Switzerland, where they enjoyed skiing and bobsledding, and Hemingway worked on articles for the *Toronto Star* to supplement the income from Hadley's trust fund. Three weeks later, they were back in Paris and settled in the apartment that Anderson's friend the translator and journalist Lewis Galantière had helped them find.

Hemingway may, in later years, have exaggerated the extent of his poverty during the years of his Paris apprenticeship somewhat, painting in *A Moveable Feast* and elsewhere a romanticized picture of the 'belly-empty, hollow-hungry' artist who subsisted on bread and pocketfuls of nuts and fruit.[43] His portrayal of himself as a diligent worker honing his craft, however, is supported not only by his accounts in his regular correspondence of having worked well that day, but by the rapid and drastic improvement in his writing that took place once he settled in Paris. He rented rooms in hotels to use as work space or occupied tables in quiet neighbourhood cafés that had little in common with the noisier Dôme and Rotonde frequented by the bohemian crowd who wanted 'to be seen publicly'.[44]

While Hemingway's juvenilia and his newspaper work demonstrate some of the same themes and stylistic traits of his mature fiction, in those early Paris years he would teach himself the 'craft of omission' – how to put crucial elements of plot beneath the surface of a story.[45] He was also learning to pare down dialogue, to drop similes in favour of concrete images, to abandon adverbs almost entirely and, when adjectives were necessary, to place them in the predicate. 'I knew I must write a novel', he recalls in *A Moveable Feast*. 'But it seemed an impossible thing to do when I had been trying with great difficulty to write paragraphs that would be the distillation of what made a novel.'[46]

For the time being, he focused on shorter pieces, and within months of his arrival in Paris was able to place some poetry in 'little magazines' – literary magazines with small audiences that self-consciously styled themselves as alternatives to the mass-market slicks. These earliest publications included 'Ultimately', a poem published in the New Orleans-based little magazine *The Double Dealer* in June 1922, and a collection of six poems grouped under the title 'Wanderings' in the January 1923 issue of *Poetry: A Magazine of Verse*, a respected Chicago publication. Anderson, with ties to the literary scene in New Orleans and a personal friend of *Poetry* editor Harriet Monroe, likely had something to do with the unknown author's successful placements. Hemingway would continue to place the occasional poem in little magazines throughout the 1920s, but he was far less interested in writing poetry than he was in mastering the skills he needed to complete a novel. Poetry served him merely as a necessary exercise of his apprenticeship and as a way of getting his name into the little magazines.[47]

When he and Hadley crossed the ocean in 1922, Hemingway left behind his earliest attempts at commercial fiction, but he did pack the beginnings of a novel he was writing about the war in Italy, which he still hoped to complete. The words weren't coming easily to him though, and he began working on smaller pieces – short stories and sketches. After months of work, only a few pieces had seen the light of day: Gertrude Stein had declared his short story 'Up in Michigan', a story of rape written from the woman's point of view, to be unpublishable, so Hemingway set it aside; he sent copies of 'My Old Man', a story considered by many critics to be both an imitation of and a challenge to his mentor Sherwood Anderson, to a *Star* colleague and to fellow newspaperman Lincoln Steffens; and he had a few short pieces and poems out to little magazines. Otherwise most of his output from that first year in Paris was unfinished and unseen.

Then, on 2 December 1922, Hemingway suffered what was simultaneously a disastrous setback and a miraculous opportunity.

Hadley, who was en route to join Hemingway in Lausanne, Switzerland, where her husband had been covering a peace conference, packed all of his works in progress so that he could work on them on their vacation. She meant to surprise him, and she certainly did. While she stepped away from the train for a few moments in the Paris Gare de Lyon, a thief stole the suitcase containing the manuscripts and carbon copies. One can only imagine the thief's chagrin at discovering his prize contained manila folders stuffed with typescripts, carbon copies and manuscripts – it would have paled, however, to Hemingway's reaction when he heard the news. As Hemingway relates in *A Moveable Feast*, he met Hadley's train in Lausanne to find her sobbing uncontrollably. He reports in the memoir that he returned to Paris immediately, though, more likely, and less dramatically, he probably did not make the trip until mid-January, and around this time the couple conceived their first child.[48] When Hemingway did arrive in Paris, his search of the apartment confirmed that his year's work was indeed gone. 'I remember what I did in the night after I let myself into the flat and found it was true,' he writes in *A Moveable Feast*, though what he did goes unstated, and he equivocates on whether the loss was instructive or destructive: 'It was probably good for me to lose early work', he said, 'trying to lie', but as he said it, 'I knew that it was true.'[49]

With the slate wiped clean, Hemingway was now forced to take Stein's advice, which she had given upon reading the now-lost novel: 'Begin over again and concentrate.'[50]

3

In Another Country, 1922–5

Although Hemingway is now considered one of the defining
personalities of literary Paris in the 1920s, residual Midwestern
values and a dislike of pretension – and, perhaps, his own
insecurities – made him leery of the art crowd that populated
Montparnasse. In a humorous article for the *Toronto Star* in March
1922, Hemingway wrote that the 'scum of Greenwich Village, New
York, has been skimmed off and deposited in large ladlesful on
that section of Paris adjacent to the Cafe Rotonde'. The crowd there
came to see and be seen, and Hemingway compared the carefully
cultivated 'careless individuality' of the patrons to the preening
and squawking of animals in a zoo exhibit. No 'real artists' were
to be found there and little 'good poetry' can be written in cafés,
Hemingway claimed – even as he had yet to prove himself as any
kind of writer other than newspaperman.[1]

Indeed, this identity as a journalist was perhaps a way for
Hemingway to safeguard his ethos, both as a man providing for the
wife whose trust fund actually kept them solvent and as someone
who worked at a day job. If he didn't publish anything right away,
he might have told himself, it was because he was on assignment
for the *Star* and not because he was the sort of loafer who had
come to Paris to spend days in the café discussing the spirit of the
age and enjoying the favourable exchange rate. In *A Moveable Feast*,
Hemingway pokes fun at himself for falling into just such a role:
when a would-be critic spies him at work and asks, 'What are you

trying to do? Write in a café?', the question highlights the pretension of the act, but the author quickly employs a corrective, moving his work home to his own table.[2] Whether or not his initial disdain for the Rotonde was, too, a kind of pose, Hemingway was careful not to give himself over to the lively social scene. As he wrote to his parents shortly after arriving in Paris, 'We know a good batch of people now in Paris and if we allowed it would have all our time taken up socially.' Anticipating their concern (and responding to their earlier charges of laziness and wasted opportunities), he assured them: 'I am working very hard.'[3]

He would maintain this scepticism of the Paris literary scene even as he insinuated himself into it. That same letter to his parents also reports, proudly, that they had had Gertrude Stein over for dinner and that she liked his poetry. His publication of poetry and other short pieces in the magazines of Paris in the 1920s was necessary to establish his legitimacy as a creative writer, so he cultivated friendships with writers, editors and publishers in that scene and was happy to name-drop to the folks back home. However, in addition to critical acclaim, he sought popular success, and his realization of that goal is one reason that Hemingway is often left out of today's critical discussions of literary modernism that include contemporaries like Pound or T. S. Eliot. Before Hemingway could make the leap from little magazine to New York publisher, and from journalist to author, however, he still had to discover his own style and narrative voice.

The suitcase theft had opened up the opportunity, and that spring Hemingway was finally able to write something new. 'My Old Man' had been an ending, not a beginning. The story – about a boy who discovers, moments after his father's death, that his old man, an ageing jockey, had been fixing races – was the culmination of the work Hemingway had been doing in Petoskey and Chicago. With its chatty first-person narrator, it reads like the slick fiction Hemingway had tried and failed to imitate in those first few months after returning from Italy. The story was stylistically sound enough that it was selected for inclusion in Small, Maynard & Company's *The Best Short Stories of 1923*, but with its O. Henry-esque twist ending, it did not yet contain the emotional slow burn of his mature fiction (and editor Edward J. O'Brien misspelled Hemingway's name in both the dedication and the byline).[4] 'Up in Michigan', the other story that pre-dates the suitcase theft, had also, in earlier drafts, suffered from a prurient 'gotcha' moment in which the author reveals that Liz had got pregnant from the encounter with Jim and later married him. Hemingway's revisions omitted this conclusion.[5]

It is 'Out of Season', however, the first short story Hemingway completed after the suitcase theft, that represents the young author's initial experiment with a 'new theory' in writing that 'you could omit anything if you knew that you omitted' and doing so would 'strengthen the story and make people feel something more than they understood'.[6] Hemingway later claimed that he omitted the detail that the local guide killed himself, but the claim does not hold up to scrutiny.[7] What the reader does sense in the quasi-autobiographical story, however, is the frustration of the right things happening at the wrong time – a disappointing trip made in wintertime to a summer resort hotel and an unplanned pregnancy the struggling author was not yet ready for lurk beneath the surface.

Each of these three early stories, then, represents an important aspect of Hemingway's transition to professional author: 'My Old Man' is Hemingway's first successful attempt to write polished fiction, and the revisions to 'Up in Michigan' demonstrate the writer's developing confidence in letting part of the narrative reside underneath the surface. This theory of omission is then further realized in 'Out of Season'. Visible in these stories are elements of the style that would characterize Hemingway's spare yet emotionally charged prose style for the rest of his career. They also contain the nascent themes that would appear again and again in his work: that life is a fixed race, that pregnancy is punishment and that insider knowledge is the privilege of very few. Together they anchor Hemingway's first book-length publication (though it might more accurately be called a chapbook), *Three Stories and Ten Poems* (1923), published by the American poet Robert McAlmon's Contact Publishing Co. in an edition of 300 copies.

Hemingway was, at this time, also at work on a series of sketches that would be published in the *Little Review* and would later make up six of the vignettes of *in our time* (1924). As he had done in 'Out of Season', the author works to convey the raw emotion of a scene through spare and objective description rather than through exposition. This famous economy of style was not merely the result of paring down weighty first drafts but was just as often the result of building up a fragment of an idea from its essential element – starting with 'one true sentence' and moving forwards from there.[8] These vignettes are significant not only in their modernist sensibility of fragmentation – Hemingway is doing something similar here to what Pound and other Imagists had done in poetry or Paul Cézanne had done in painting – but because they represent Hemingway's first real success in writing about the war.

The abandoned – and then lost – first novel had been an attempt to write about the war, but with the vignettes of *in our time* Hemingway claims his first success at portraying both the violence and the impersonality that characterized the mechanized warfare and tangled alliances of the Great War. One key to his success was in abandoning, for a time, the attempts to write from his own experience in the Red Cross. Instead, he draws from his knowledge of war gleaned from his extensive reading and his conversations with veterans like Eric Edward 'Chink' Dorman-Smith, a young British officer whom Hemingway had met at the hospital in Milan. Thus he is able to capture scenes outside his own limited experience on the Italian front with such detached attention to detail that readers often assume, wrongly, that he had witnessed these events at first hand.

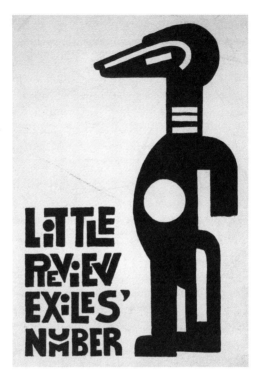

The Little Review was one of the most influential of the English-language 'little magazines' published in Paris. In the Spring 1923 issue Hemingway published six vignettes that would later be included in *in our time* (1924).

Dorman-Smith is regarded as the source or inspiration for the third vignette, for example, which gives a brief glimpse at one of the war's earliest engagements. At only 75 words long, the first-person account exhibits a bemused nonchalance about 'pott[ing]' German soldiers as they scramble, one by one, over a wall. The paragraph conveys the emotional detachment of the narrator, the ignominious death of the Germans and the contrast between nature (the 'garden at Mons') and the man-made weapons. A closer look reveals religious symbolism as well: the German solider '*fell* down into the *garden*' (emphasis added). Awareness of the precise historical moment – the collection is, after all, called *in our time* – adds even more layers of significance to the deceptively simple form of the vignette.[9] Hemingway's contemporaries would have recognized Mons as the first major engagement of the British Expeditionary Forces on the Western Front, a battle in which 70,000 volunteer infantrymen went up against more than 200,000 Germans, but, having a better defensive position, the British were able to administer heavy casualties to the Germans before finally falling back. Thus this engagement represents for Hemingway's contemporary readers the mythos of the war as a 'noble sacrifice'. Hemingway's vignette, in which death is doled out mechanically, almost comically and certainly not nobly – either for the shooter or for the surprised Germans who drop to the ground – creates an 'ironic counter-myth', rejecting platitudes of both the glories *and* the horrors of war.[10]

War is, in Chapter Three, the impersonal 'potting' of one soldier by another; it makes for an amusing anecdote. Yet the narrators of the vignettes may encounter, as does Nick in Chapter Six, 'a disappointing audience' unable to hear the story, or, in the case of the narrator of Chapter Seven, he may ultimately decide to tell no one at all.[11] The common motif of violence throughout the vignettes of war, bullfighting and crime is not the only connecting thread; the vignettes are, too, an account of the difficulty of storytelling.

'On the Quai at Smyrna', added to the collection as an introduction beginning with the Scribner's edition of 1930 but probably written four or more years earlier, drives home this point.[12] The vignette recalls the razing of Greek-occupied Smyrna by the Turks in 1922, during which British forces, operating under a policy of neutrality, stood by as Greek refugees poured onto the waterfront. The unidentified narrator relates a second unnamed narrator's eyewitness account. This second teller recalls his mediation of a misunderstanding between a Turkish officer and a British gunner's mate, and how he handled the misunderstanding by creating a fiction for the insulted Turkish officer, assuring him that the offending gunner's mate would be 'most severely dealt with'.[13] With pronouns in all three points of view – 'I', 'he' and 'you' – none of which have antecedents, but with several layers of indirect discourse and acknowledgement of the fallibility of translation and cultural differences, the account does more than offer a portrait of the toll of total war and its subsequent failed diplomacy; it acknowledges the impossibility of ever accurately telling that story. The vignette demonstrates the impact of abstract politics on everyday people, with the British officer's comforting lies reflecting the British government's promised alliance with Greece, which the British failed to support militarily when the Turks razed the city.[14] Hemingway's lifelong distrust of government, which may have been born out of a run-in with a game warden in adolescence, was cemented by what he witnessed as a correspondent reporting from the various conferences that followed the end of the war.[15] Yet these arguments remain beneath the surface, as the impact of the dead babies, stiff corpses and drowned pack animals of the vignette is sublimated by the narrative deferrals, so that it all becomes, as the inured speaker declares with detached irony, a 'most pleasant business'.[16]

For Hemingway, the vignettes that went into the 'Exile's Number' of the *Little Review* in 1923 and began *in our time* were hard won. He had struggled since arriving in Paris to make a name for himself among the Left Bank literati, and these pieces were the first real success of that apprenticeship. However, he still needed a book, and, for Hemingway, vanity presses and small presses like Robert McAlmon's Contact Editions or Bill Bird's Three Mountains Press hardly counted. What Hemingway wanted was to see his work in print with a major New York publisher. Before that could happen, however, he would need to produce a novel, or, at the very least, a full collection of stories.

Change was afoot in Hemingway's life – both personally and professionally – and the years 1923–5 represent a flurry of activity. In January 1923 *Poetry* had billed him as 'a young Chicago poet now abroad who will soon issue in Paris his first book of verse'.[17] By the end of that summer, however, he had stopped dabbling in poetry, and, having witnessed his first bullfighting season in Spain, was rounding out his collection of vignettes for *in our time* with a series of bullfighting sketches. Hemingway updated Pound on his progress turning the vignettes into a book of substance:

> The bulls start. then reapear and then finish off. The war starts clear and noble just like it did, Mons etc., gets close and blurred and finished with the feller who goes home and gets clap . . . It has form all right.[18]

This new work would free him for good from any association he had with poetry, or with Chicago – and with the little magazines for that matter. He was becoming Ernest Hemingway, a cosmopolitan writer of innovative fiction.

In August 1923, just as his career was starting to build a little momentum, the Hemingways moved to Toronto, where Hemingway went to work full time at the *Star*. The reasons behind the move are not entirely clear. The eight-months-pregnant Hadley was glad to deliver her baby in a well-equipped Anglophone hospital, but the move had been planned before Hadley even knew of her pregnancy.[19] The move to Canada may have served as a sort of self-imposed terminus to Hemingway's stint as an expatriate, but, as Hemingway had plans to eventually return to France, it was more likely a temporary relocation to set aside a little extra money and to gain a change of scenery.[20] In any case, if he hadn't made it as a writer by the time his Canadian contract started, he at least had a job in journalism waiting. Perhaps the idea of returning to Canada, a location which he told Ezra Pound shortly after his arrival 'couldn't be any worse', was meant to serve as a motivating factor to make the fiction career work.[21] By the time the planned move came around, though, *Three Stories and Ten Poems* was on the shelf at

Sylvia Beach's bookshop, and Bill Bird was in possession of the vignettes of *in our time*. The move back to Toronto proved an interruption – not a motivation – and Hemingway worked long hours on unsigned pieces for the paper while his fiction writing languished. Within four months, Hemingway had had enough. He quit the *Star*, and the trio – baby John Hadley Nicanor Hemingway, nicknamed Bumby, had been born on 10 October 1923 – returned to Paris shortly after the New Year.

Perhaps Toronto had been good motivation after all, in that it had been a trip to Hades and back, but Hemingway would not make the classic mistake of looking over his shoulder, for he had every intention of leaving. He had made a quick and obligatory solo trek out to Oak Park before sailing to France – it was the last time he would see his father alive – but once he got back to Paris, Hemingway paid little heed to the conservative American values that kept Joyce's *Ulysses* off the shelves on his parents' side of the Atlantic. He also told Gertrude Stein he planned 'to chuck journalism', as she had ruined him for it anyway.[22] He had laboured slowly over his vignettes the previous year, but now he wrote one short story after another. Free of his American ties, he was finally able to write about Michigan lakes and rivers, the complicated relationship between young Nick Adams and his father, and between Doctor Adams and his wife. None of his coterie publications, however, paid him enough to live on, and Hadley's trust fund was no longer bringing in quite as much as it once had. Ostensibly happy in his own marriage – no other woman had yet come between them – Hemingway nevertheless produced during this period what scholars, Carlos Baker first among them, have noted is a sort of 'marriage-group' of tales.[23] In these stories, husbands and wives fail to communicate and suffer from being trapped by social convention and by biology.

In 'The Doctor and the Doctor's Wife', Nick Adams's father, feeling emasculated by a verbal altercation with a larger man, a 'half-breed' Native American – or a white man passing as such – whom he had hired for an odd job, engages in a conversation with his wife that proves equally enervating as she presses him for the details of the argument.[24] The wife's Christian Science reading material alerts the reader to conflict in this marriage; a tenet of the Christian Scientist faith is the adherents' rejection of mainstream medical treatments in favour of prayer, a circumstance at odds with the doctor's profession and, given the title of the story, his very identity. The tension between the two is palpable as the seething doctor goes into his room and loads and reloads his shotgun. Observant readers will note, too, that the doctor's wife's window is open at the end of the story, as she calls out to her husband; the open window would have allowed her to hear the argument between the two men, making her questions for the doctor not actual questions so much as taunts, as she forces him to revisit the scene of his unmanning.[25]

In 'Cross-Country Snow', the young husband is ambivalent about his wife's pregnancy, and he knows that his new role as father will restrict him from pursuing future skiing trips with his friend. Meanwhile, the title characters of 'Mr and Mrs Elliot' are troubled with the opposite problem – the sexually inexperienced Mr Elliot and his older wife 'tried very hard' to have a baby, but proved unsuccessful.[26] The brief experiment with heterosexual domesticity thwarted by unfortunate biology, their marriage takes an unconventional form, with Cornelia's female friend joining her in the marriage bed and Hubert giving himself over, instead, to the writing of poetry, which he then pays to publish.

Undoubtedly some elements in the stories are drawn straight from Hemingway's own life: Hemingway did not bother to change the names of several Walloon Lake locals in 'The Doctor and the Doctor's Wife'; Mr and Mrs Elliot satirize a real-life expatriate poet, Chard Powers Smith, a point so obvious that it necessitated a name change (from Smith to Elliot) before the story was published in the

Little Review. But these stories are not journalistic retellings of real-life events.[27] Hemingway borrows from real people and real experiences as a starting point, but the structure of the stories and the details chosen, omitted and manipulated are carefully crafted fiction. That neither Hemingway's greatest fans nor his harshest critics can absolve him of having simply set his own life into prose is a testament to his success in creating emotional truths too real to be disbelieved, a success that nevertheless needled the writer who lamented: 'The point is I want them all to sound as though they really happened. Then when I succeed those poor dumb pricks say they are all just skillful reporting.'[28]

Hemingway was well aware that his use of real people and places might be misconstrued. In a particularly metatextual moment that Hemingway eventually cut from 'Big Two-Hearted River', the writer muses that 'the only writing that was any good was what you made up, what you imagined . . . Nick in the stories was never himself.'[29] Hemingway isn't Nick, and as this story insists, Nick was not Nick either, but the temptation to read Hemingway's life through his fiction when Nick reflects on having written stories that bear unmistakable resemblance to those in *In Our Time* is irresistible. How can readers reconcile Hemingway's use of his avatar in an unmistakably autobiographical passage with his denial of that very usage? Why should we believe him – Nick or Hemingway – when the self-portrait seems so clearly drawn and the speaker so ambiguous?

It is worth noting that the stories that have proven most tempting to biographers looking to mine Hemingway's fiction for insight into his life are the ones that went unpublished during his lifetime: *A Moveable Feast*, never completed and published posthumously; the passage cut from 'Big Two-Hearted River' and published posthumously as 'On Writing'; and manuscript fragments of early drafts, like that of 'A Very Short Story' or 'Now I Lay Me', that bear a closer resemblance to their models than do the published pieces.[30] These were stories that Hemingway had yet to finish and represent a liminal space between the life and the art. *A Moveable Feast* must be handled with particular care because, though it serves as Hemingway's memoir, he insists in page after compulsively reworked page of the manuscript that the book is fiction. The oft-quoted preface to the edition from 1964 that equivocates 'if the reader prefers [the] book may be regarded as fiction' was cobbled together from manuscript fragments.[31] In the manuscripts, however, Hemingway is adamant in his refusal to own the work as non-fiction. The remembered life, too, is fiction. If it was an autobiography at all, it was done by 'remate', a term Hemingway borrowed from the sport of jai alai and which denoted a 'double-wall rebound'.[32]

Many voices, then, work to tell Hemingway's story: the archival record, the fiction and Hemingway himself, as well as the other memoirs of Paris that bear competing, contradictory accounts of people, places and events. The story that emerges from all of these sources, however, is that the 1920s in Paris was a time of changes, and 1925 – the year that saw the publication of F. Scott Fitzgerald's *The Great Gatsby*, Stein's *The Making of Americans* and Virginia Woolf's *Mrs Dalloway* – was a watershed year for modernism and for Hemingway. With his first short story cycle complete, Hemingway was looking for a publisher, and he was determined to venture outside the Latin Quarter to find one.

4

The End of Something, 1925–6

Hemingway had managed to generate some buzz for himself with his contributions to the little magazines and the two slight volumes published in Paris, reviewed favourably in *The Dial* by influential critic Edmund Wilson.[1] The buzz was not merely the result of these successes: in letters to friends, and, undoubtedly, in conversation around the Quarter, Hemingway let it be known that he was seeking a New York publisher for his first book of short stories. Well-connected friends and acquaintances plugged the collection for him at Doran, at Knopf and at Boni & Liveright. Unbeknownst to Hemingway, F. Scott Fitzgerald – the author of *This Side of Paradise* (1920) and of short stories appearing in the *Saturday Evening Post* – read *in our time* and liked what he found. Though he had yet to become personally acquainted with Hemingway, he wrote to Maxwell Perkins, his editor at Charles Scribner's Sons, that the young expatriate had 'a brilliant future' and that Perkins should 'look him up right away'.[2] Perkins had been influential in opening up the conservative Scribner's lists to modernist voices, and, on Fitzgerald's recommendation, he procured a copy of *in our time*. Favourably impressed, Perkins sent Hemingway a letter of interest requesting that he submit a manuscript for consideration.[3]

Unfortunately, it took weeks for Perkins to receive, read and respond to *in our time*, and his letter, held with other mail at Sylvia Beach's shop, did not reach Hemingway in Austria, where he and Hadley had gone to ski. Meanwhile, Boni & Liveright got through to

Hemingway first, cabling him directly with a firm offer. Hemingway, ready for an American publisher, responded in turn 'DELIGHTED TO ACCEPT'.[4] The $200 advance against royalties was his biggest payday to that point, and, as the home of Sherwood Anderson and Harold Loeb, the publishing house, along with the contract it offered, was respectable enough to please any up-and-coming author of literary fiction. Nevertheless, one can imagine Hemingway's likely disappointment and frustration when he returned to Paris that March and found Perkins's letter waiting for him. He told Perkins in his belated reply that he would have been glad to send Scribner's the manuscript of *In Our Time*.[5] At the very least, he could have leveraged the publisher's interest to negotiate better terms.

Still, Boni & Liveright was a good fit for an innovative modernist writer. Afloat on the profits from its Modern Library series of affordable classics, Boni & Liveright was able to take some risks with experimental work coming in from expatriates in Europe.[6] What Liveright wanted 'most of all', he explained to Ezra Pound in 1920, were 'really good novels which at the same time have some popular appeal'.[7] Having read the stories delivered to him by Loeb, Liveright saw in Hemingway the potential for just such a novel.

That novel did not yet exist, and Hemingway was increasingly aware of the necessity of producing it. Nevertheless, he told Perkins that he didn't care to write a novel, preferring to focus on short stories and, 'some day', to write 'a sort of Daughty's Arabia Deserta of the Bull Ring, a very big book with some wonderful pictures'.[8] His disinterest may have stemmed from his own shortcomings: the lost novel about the Italian front was not worth recreating. His stated desire to write a book about bullfighting was premature – it would be the better part of a decade before he published *Death in the Afternoon*, his compendium on the sport, in 1932. As it turned out though, bullfighting did figure heavily in his first novel, which sprang onto the page in less than three months following

Untitled watercolour by John Dos Passos that depicts Hemingway (left) at the *novillada* (amateur bullfight) during the festival of San Fermín in Pamplona, 1924.

Hemingway's now-legendary trip in 1925 with friends to the festival of San Fermín in Pamplona, Spain.

The Hemingways had been to Pamplona twice before, in 1923 and 1924, and as they made plans to return yet again in July 1925, they anticipated the same rowdy mix of bullfighting, drinking and dancing at the provincial festival that they had experienced in the previous two years. They got what they came for, but this time the bullfighting and carousing would be set against a backdrop of sexual tension and jealousy. The disappointment of the *feria* provided the inspiration that Hemingway needed to finally write his war novel: 'There are no drawn battles in bull fighting', Hemingway came to understand upon first discovering the sport, or, rather, the 'tragedy'.[9] The bull was, before it even entered the ring, destined to die. What mattered was the way it died, an idea that resonates in *The Sun Also Rises* and in Hemingway's works to come.

The Sun Also Rises is narrated by Jake Barnes, an expatriate American working as a journalist in Paris, and it follows Jake and a group of friends from Paris to Pamplona. There tensions rise as Robert Cohn, a modestly successful novelist, tries to ingratiate himself with the beautiful, hard-drinking Brett Ashley, with whom he has had a brief affair. Brett takes up with a bullfighting prodigy, Pedro Romero. Tempers flare, astonishing amounts of alcohol are consumed, and Jake's own passion for Brett is barely contained. In the novel's famous last exchange, Brett tells Jake they 'could have had such a damned good time together', to which he replies, 'Yes . . . Isn't it pretty to think so?'[10]

It was a novel of dissipated youth and of the walking wounded, with Jake's wounds representing the invisible, yet indelible, effects of war. Outwardly, Jake seems whole, but despite his interest in rituals of masculinity – fly fishing and the bullfight – like the Fisher King of medieval legend or the steers who calm the fighting bulls, Jake has been rendered impotent. The text suggests, though it does not declare it outright, that Jake lost his penis while flying aircraft in Italy. It is 'a rotten way to be wounded', he avers.[11] Not a eunuch, Jake experiences sexual desire, but he is unable to act upon it. There are other wounds in the novel as well: during the war, Brett had served in a Voluntary Aid Detachment, nursing the wounded and witnessing at first hand the horrors of war. To take Brett at her word and to see her as a 'bitch' or to see her as a prize to be won – by Cohn, Romero or, in his imagination, Jake – is to overlook Brett's own trauma.[12] Though nurses did not 'see battle', as the euphemism for combat puts it, the effects of war were the focal point for those women whose task it was to treat the wounded.[13] Brett, an unmarriageable drunk, is a casualty of war who bears the 'shared but unspoken trauma' with Jake and the rest of their generation.[14] *The Sun Also Rises* demonstrates the effects of war not only on the corporeal body (Jake) but on the family body (Brett). Brett explains her refusal to marry Romero: 'I'm not going to be one of these bitches that ruins children.'[15] Cohn, whose combat experience is the artificial combat of organized sport – the novel opens with the information that he 'was once middleweight boxing champion of Princeton' – lacks this shared experience, and that naivety makes him appealing to Brett and hateful to Jake.[16] Cohn is Jake's foil. As readers of the first-person narrative told through Jake's perspective, we are led to understand Cohn through anti-Semitic stereotypes; he is effete and a hanger-on. In actuality, it is Jake who is rootless, who has 'lost touch with the soil'.[17] And it is Jake who cannot consummate a sexual relationship and who obsesses over money.[18]

Jake is not a hero, nor is he Hemingway, yet readers eagerly made connections between the characters in the book and their real-life models: Harold Loeb, author of the novel *Doodab* (1925) and one of the friends who had foisted Hemingway's work onto Horace Liveright, inspired Robert Cohn, also Jewish and also a novelist enjoying some minor success. The British socialite Mary 'Duff' Stirling, Lady Twysden, inspired the character Brett Ashley, who was 'built with curves like the hull of a racing yacht'.[19] Like Duff, who was engaged to one Pat Guthrie, Brett has a Scottish fiancé, Mike Campbell. Bill Gorton, Jake's friend and fishing buddy, sounds a great deal like Bill Smith, Hemingway's friend and sometime flatmate from the Michigan and Chicago days. And Jake Barnes, 'Hem' in the earliest manuscripts – and even as 'I' in an outline for the book – was, like Hemingway, an expatriate living in Paris and working as a journalist. Other real-life personages appear, loosely disguised, in the book as well.[20] Noticeably missing from the novel, however, is Hadley; Jake Barnes has no wife.

It would be easy to imagine Hemingway wishing Hadley out of existence and recreating the unconsummated desire for Duff as an impossible love between Jake and Brett, but there is little evidence to suggest the relationship between Hemingway and Duff was ever more than a one-sided, unrequited crush. Loeb, however, did have a brief fling with Duff, and his mooning over her, her fiancé's understandable irritation and Hemingway's jealous mood tempered the joviality of the group. The tensions that arose in Pamplona between the friends are unimportant now. They simply provided the starting point for the novel that is much more than a roman-à-clef, a how-to manual of dissipation for would-be flaming youth or the manifesto of a so-called 'lost generation'.

In hotels in Madrid and Valencia, where Hemingway and Hadley had gone on alone to take in more bullfights, Hemingway began the novel. By the end of that summer, he had made substantial headway on the book, which he was now calling *Fiesta*. His confidence growing, he began to show signs of discontent with Boni & Liveright.

In a letter to Jane Heap, editor of the *Little Review*, from August 1925, Hemingway notes that he is no longer satisfied writing vignettes and short stories, and he expresses a desire to be like Tolstoy, who found perfection in the long form. This admission leads directly to a paragraph about Boni & Liveright's bringing out *In Our Time*, slated for publication in October, and he gives Heap the details of his contract. Specifically, the contract gave the publisher an option on Hemingway's next three books, at least one of which was to be a novel, but, in what would turn out to be a significant clause of the contract, the document also notes that 'unless we publish your second book, we relinquish our option on the third book'.[21]

After his explanation to Heap of the contract, the letter breaks off: someone has torn part of the page completely off. Because the resulting page fragments are numbered in the same ink the letter is written in and numbered in Hemingway's hand, that someone was obviously Hemingway himself.[22] When the letter picks back up, Hemingway cautions that he can't yet talk about business but that he's going to hold out for a big advance on the new book because he's put in too much work for almost no financial reward, and now that he's got a desirable product, he's not going to sell himself short.

The letter to Heap shows that Hemingway wanted to be another Tolstoy, and he may have already been sceptical of Boni & Liveright's ability to make that happen. He may also have already been hatching a plan to see to it that the publisher didn't even get a chance. What was written on the torn-away sheet will never be

Portrait of Ernest Hemingway by his mother, Grace Hall Hemingway, *c.* 1925, after a 1923 photo by Man Ray.

known, but in the months that followed Hemingway would slip out of the Boni & Liveright contract and join Scribner's, who would remain his publisher for the rest of his life.

Hemingway's concerns about the marketing of his forthcoming book proved valid. Few reviews preceded the publication of *In Our Time*, indicating that the publisher may not have circulated review copies, and the cover, which was crowded with blurbs by Sherwood Anderson, Edward J. O'Brien, Gilbert Seldes, Ford Madox Ford, Waldo Frank and Donald Ogden Stewart, seemed to Hemingway to be trying too hard. The campaign relied almost exclusively on using solicited endorsements of literary insiders rather than selling the book on its own merits. The Boni & Liveright catalogue, too, pushed the book by associating Hemingway with other established authors, again name-dropping Anderson and Ford, as well as comparing the author to Joyce and Pound.[23]

Liveright certainly wasn't trying to keep *In Our Time* out of the hands of readers, but the publisher had realistic expectations for its saleability. Liveright wrote to Hemingway that the author was 'a property' and the publishing house 'builders' – he seemed to be holding out for a future novel before investing heavily in an advertising campaign.[24] It was a self-fulfilling prophecy perhaps, but Liveright was correct in his low sales expectations – *In Our Time* did not sell out the first printing of only 1,335 copies.[25] Though sales were slow, Liveright saw the value of the book as an example of modernist experimentation, and what publicity it did receive traded on that pedigree.

Adverts for the book in the *New York Times Book Review* touted *In Our Time* as 'utterly *new* stories in a new way with a new simplicity' – a refrain that situated the work firmly in the modernist movement.[26] The connection between the marketing of the book and its identity as a product of highbrow modernist literature was not lost on reviewers: 'The praise of such men [like Ford and Anderson] . . . implies that his work is experimental, original, modernistic.'[27]

Liveright defended this marketing strategy, writing to Hemingway, 'You must realize that the little group in America that read some of your work in the highbrow magazines amounts to very little in the sale of a book.'[28] The letter echoes a letter to Pound from 1923 in which Liveright had lamented, 'Do you suppose I like to go on losing money on you miserable highbrows? But no matter what you write, you know I always want to publish your poetry and I know that I do and will do more for it than anyone else.'[29] Where Liveright made his crucial misstep was that, while he understood Hemingway to be an author with a future, he failed to see that, in 1925, highbrow was trickling down into something new and marketable: the middlebrow. In treating *In Our Time* as modernistic (and thus unsellable), Boni & Liveright misread both the marketplace and Hemingway's ambition.

Hemingway, an innovative author who nevertheless wanted to write best-sellers, was just the kind of author this aspirational consumer culture demanded. By the mid-1920s, modernism had gone mainstream – it was 'difficult but not unapproachable, different but not unrecognizable' – and this balance between the difficult and the accessible characterized Hemingway's work.[30] 'My book will be praised by highbrows and can be read by lowbrows', Hemingway told Liveright. 'There is no writing in [*In Our Time*] that anybody with a high-school education cannot read', and yet the book was not simple.[31]

Hemingway knew that *Fiesta* was good, and he did not want to risk bringing it out with Boni & Liveright, whom he blamed for the lacklustre sales of *In Our Time*. Though the archival record suggests that Hemingway was careful never to indicate in writing that there was anything at all calculated about the way in which he changed publishers, Hemingway likely wrote the satirical novella *The Torrents of Spring* (1926) for one main reason: to produce a book that Liveright would have no choice but to decline, thus freeing him from his contractual obligations.

Though it still needed major revisions, *Fiesta* was essentially complete when Hemingway pounded out *Torrents* in less than two weeks. The book poked fun at the literary stylings (and pretensions) of his contemporaries, especially Anderson and Stein, and its stream-of-consciousness narrative conveniently allowed Hemingway to compose the book off the top of his head.

When he submitted the novella to Liveright, Hemingway straight-facedly wrote that it had the potential to be a modern classic and the first great American satire. In his letter, Hemingway offers suggestions on typesetting and illustration as if he imagines the book going to press, but he also plants the idea of its necessary rejection: 'The only reason I can conceive that you might not want to publish it would be for fear of offending Sherwood.'[32] Liveright had to choose, and, as Hemingway knew, he would choose Anderson, whose *Dark Laughter* had sold 30,000 copies to the 1,083 of *In Our Time*.

Liveright cabled the anticipated rejection and indicated eagerness to see *The Sun Also Rises*, as the draft was now called. Instead of acting on Liveright's request, Hemingway made arrangements to get *Torrents* to Scribner's – Scribner's, in turn, would publish the book in May of 1926, quickly following up in October with *Sun*.

Hemingway sounded gleeful, even defiant, when he described the terms of the now-broken contract to Fitzgerald: 'So I'm loose. No matter what Horace may think up in his letter to say . . . I have known all along that they could not and would not be able to publish it as it makes a bum out of their present ace and best seller Anderson.' Almost as an afterthought, Hemingway adds, unconvincingly, 'I did not, however, have that in mind in any way when I wrote it.'[33]

It seems counter-intuitive that Hemingway, whose only major publication was a book of short stories, who wanted to publish a novel and who had in the can what he knew was a groundbreaking first novel, would instead offer up to the American public a smaller book that lambasted middle America, American literature and his own publisher. But all along Hemingway wanted to exchange the insular expatriate scene for a wider readership. He wanted money. He wanted advertising. He wanted best-sellers. He wanted glowing reviews. And he wanted all that without compromising his artistic vision.

Perhaps Liveright was susceptible to the same belief in a 'great divide' that for so long dominated the narrative modernism invented for itself, a narrative that viewed 'aesthetic virtue and commerce [as] antithetical principles' and defined modernism in terms of its opposition to the Victorian mass market.[34] This ambivalence between high and lowbrow was further complicated in the 1920s by the rapidly growing mass media, including advertising, and 'advertisements for modern literature taught consumers in the United States that modernism, like many other new products of the time, was good for them as long as they used it correctly.'[35] Liveright had tried to capture a certain modernist exclusivity with the dust jacket and promotion of *In Our Time*, but the market's resistance to the book proved all too real. Scribner's, on the other hand, heavily promoted Hemingway while positioning him as a fresh, new voice out of Europe that was criticizing the other, formerly fresh, new voices. In striking just the right balance, and appealing to the emergent middlebrow, the strategy of Scribner's worked where Boni & Liveright's had not.

Scribner's approached *Torrents* in exactly the right manner, positioning it against modernism by contextualizing it in promotional materials as a

revolt against the soft, vague thought and expression that characterizes the work of the extremists in American fiction today . . . a burlesque of . . . literary tendencies associated with American and British writers akin to Anderson, such as D. H. Lawrence, James Joyce, John Dos Passos, etc.[36]

This announcement is especially notable because it name-drops, in a disparaging way, some of the same names that Boni & Liveright had used to promote *In Our Time*. Hemingway, the satirical book proved, was ready to move beyond the little magazines and *In Our Time*, but the reader still had to be in the know to appreciate the significance. Where Liveright had balked, Perkins took a risk – and it paid off in the long run for both author and publisher. The lucrative relationship was necessarily two-sided. As Hemingway rightly informed Liveright in his letter asserting his intention to change publishers: 'I will pay my keep to, and eventually make a great deal of money for, any publisher.'[37]

The new publisher was not the only monumental change in Hemingway's life in that watershed year. In 1925 Hemingway met the man who had recommended him to Perkins, and they quickly became friends. Fitzgerald, who was to Hemingway both a peer and a mentor, would offer editorial suggestions that did more for Hemingway's early work than any other single influence – a circumstance that necessarily doomed the friendship. As his dealings with Anderson had shown, Hemingway could not abide literary indebtedness. That year Hemingway also became acquainted with Pauline Pfeiffer, an independently wealthy fashion writer, and the girlish friendship Pauline initially cultivated with Hadley shifted into an affair with Ernest.

Hemingway had been in Austria when he got word that Boni & Liveright would publish *In Our Time*, and he was there again when he received the publisher's anticipated rejection of *The Torrents of Spring*. The little village of Schruns also saw the beginning of his affair with Pauline. Meteorological events take on special significance in Hemingway's writing, and in *A Moveable Feast* he recalls the winter of 1924–5 as 'the year that so many people were killed in avalanches'. Yet that avalanche winter was 'like a happy and innocent winter in childhood' compared to 1925–6, the beginning of the end of his marriage to Hadley.[38]

When writing *A Moveable Feast*, Hemingway struggled and failed to find in Alpine skiing the appropriate metaphor for what had happened to his relationship with Hadley: 'People break their legs and in the world some people still break their hearts.'[39] Three decades later he expressed feelings of regret, but at the time Hemingway may have seen only exciting opportunities as he set off for New York to straighten out the arrangements of changing publishers, and then, on the way back, to linger too long with Pauline in Paris.

Despite an increasingly obvious infatuation between the two, Hemingway and Pauline maintained the pretense of platonic friendship. In the summer of 1926, the trio shared lodgings on the French Riviera. The Hemingway marriage was essentially over, but Hemingway, who must have dreaded the reaction of his conservative parents to the dissolution of his marriage, carried on in his correspondence as if nothing were amiss, and he even sent his parents photographs of the family taken on the beach. They look like typical holiday photos, the parents taking turns posing with their smiling child at the water's edge.[40] Clarence and Grace had no idea that outside the frame of the photo was their next daughter-in-law, determined to win the husband for herself through a war of attrition.

Finally, it was all too much to bear, and the Hemingways decided to separate. Hemingway fictionalized the train ride that carried him and Hadley back 'to Paris to set up separate residences' in the story 'A Canary for One' (1927).[41] Sharing the train car with the couple is an American lady who is bringing a canary to her daughter as a consolation for having impelled her to break off her engagement to a European. American men, the woman declares, are the only suitable husbands. The American lady is 'a little deaf' and keeps close by the train when it stops in Marseilles because 'she was afraid that perhaps signals of departure were given and that she did not hear them'.[42] She is also deaf to the wreck she has made of her

Hemingway sent his parents this photo of himself and his son, John Hadley Nicanor 'Bumby' Hemingway, enjoying the French Riviera in July 1926. Another photo included with the letter shows Hadley cuddling their son on the beach and smiling, but in reality the marriage was failing. Pauline Pfeiffer had joined the Hemingways on this trip, and Ernest and Hadley separated shortly thereafter.

daughter's life, symbolized by the passing scenery: three wrecked train cars, and, in an even less subtle image, a house on fire. Hadley, a pianist, was not deaf, yet she too may have been deaf to the 'signals of departure' her husband had been giving her since the infatuation with Pauline had begun that winter in Schruns.

Hemingway's marriage to Hadley was not the only relationship to unravel that year. Sherwood Anderson, still smarting from the blow dealt to him by *The Torrents of Spring* and an obsequious letter from Hemingway trying to justify the book, scolded Hemingway both for the cruel satire and for Hemingway's 'patronizing' attempt to defend it: 'It must be Paris – the literary life' that had changed his old friend, Anderson concludes, surely knowing how afraid Hemingway was of losing his edge and taking on the effete affectations of the Left Bank literati.[43] Anderson was willing to put the past behind him, however, and invited the Hemingways to visit him in Virginia. Hemingway would soon head back stateside, but he would not visit Anderson, nor would Hadley accompany him.

So much had happened in a year: the contract with Boni & Liveright and his marriage vows were both broken, and the old friends – Anderson, Stein, Loeb and others – were traded for new ones in F. Scott Fitzgerald, wealthy patrons Gerald and Sara Murphy and poet Archibald MacLeish. With Hemingway's sun rising in the literary world, little remained of the earnest kid from Chicago whom Anderson had taken under his wing. In his place was a cosmopolitan professional whose celebrity would soon eclipse that of the insular group of writers who had helped him achieve it.

5

The Light of the World, 1926–9

In the autumn of 1926, Hadley devised the terms for granting Hemingway a divorce: the couple would separate, but Hadley required that Hemingway also separate himself from Pauline for a period of 100 days. She wanted all parties involved to be certain of their decision. Pauline went back to America to wait, Hadley began building a life for herself separate from – or, perhaps, free from – Hemingway, and Hemingway borrowed Gerald Murphy's Paris apartment. Driven by guilt and grief to thoughts of suicide, Hemingway filled the void by getting *The Sun Also Rises* ready for publication and putting together new stories for a collection – the appropriately titled *Men Without Women* – that would appear in autumn 1927.[1]

Hemingway's marriage may have been over, but his career had just begun. As a gesture of appreciation for the woman whose support had allowed him to write the book and whose love had been a casualty of circumstances surrounding its creation, Hemingway dedicated *The Sun Also Rises* to Hadley and their son, and assigned all royalties from its sale to her.

The book was published on 22 October 1926. Reviews of the novel were mixed, but it sold well. John Dos Passos, a friend whose *Three Soldiers* (1920) anticipates Hemingway's realistic depiction of the crushing tedium and arbitrary violence of war in *A Farewell to Arms*, praised the novel's style and its characters that were 'so vividly put down you could recognize their faces on a passport photo', but he insisted that the book lacked the substance its epigraphs – and the author's previous short stories – promised.[2] Fanny Butcher, writing for the *Chicago Tribune* (and thus for Hemingway's hometown market) also lauded Hemingway's talent as a stylist but declared that his characters were 'degraded people' of the sort one might expect from 'a mediocre young man from Oak Park, IL, and not one with real talent'.[3] The dig made Hemingway's choice of subject seem at once too coarse and too parochial for the cultured readers of Chicago. Hemingway's harshest critic was his own mother, who called the novel 'one of the filthiest books of the year'.[4] In his measured reply to his parents, which he wrote after letting his initial anger and hurt dissipate somewhat, Hemingway declares that he is 'in no way ashamed' of the book and suggests that the darker impulses in it are 'no more unpleasant' than whatever went on in the private lives of the Oak Park establishment.[5] He appeals to Grace as both a loving son and as a fellow artist, reminding his mother, who was having some success reinventing herself as a painter, that it was necessary to attempt to portray people as they really are. 'I have a long life to write other books and the subjects will not always be the same – except they will all, I hope, be human beings.'[6] Even as he defends himself and his artistic choices, he notes, with pride, that he has had requests for stories from *Vanity Fair* and *Cosmopolitan*, high-profile slicks that catered to a wide audience interested in art, literature and culture. In invoking the names of these periodicals, Hemingway demonstrates to his mother his acceptance by mainstream cultural arbiters and his ability to generate a livable income from his writing. The name-dropping serves, too, to trump his mother's own recent achievement of having one of her paintings reproduced in Marshall Field's department store catalogue. Rhetorically, the letter is a masterpiece: Hemingway's congratulations on Grace's recent work and his appeals to a shared artistic ethos appear conciliatory, but they also work as calculated attacks: what is Marshall Field & Company compared to *Vanity Fair*? And what is fictional carousing compared to a real-life divorce? Since his mother's moral sensibilities were already being tested by his work, this letter seems as good a time as any to inform his parents of his separation from Hadley, and Hemingway certainly knew that the announcement would be met with their dismay and disapproval.[7]

By now Hemingway's separations – leaving Hadley for Pauline and Boni & Liveright for Scribner's – were old news around the Quarter, and Hemingway had little stake in anything the gossips might have to say about these transitions. His apprenticeship over, Hemingway was focusing on growing his new relationships; his commitment to his publisher, at least, would prove to be lifelong. For better or for worse, Hemingway had found an advocate in editor Maxwell Perkins, who would allow him to follow a career path of his own devising. A modernist working from Paris signed to an established New York publisher, Hemingway was determined to have it both ways: to write what he wanted and to write books that people would buy – not an outlandish goal for any author of course, but, the contract-breaking *Torrents* excepted, he was willing to sacrifice neither artistry nor saleability. Scribner's, a conservative and well-known house, offered him the opportunity to publish short stories in *Scribner's Magazine*, reaching a wide audience and generating income and publicity; meanwhile, Perkins, who had worked behind the scenes to open up the lists of Scribner's to more modern talent, like F. Scott Fitzgerald and Thomas Wolfe, allowed Hemingway to write about subjects that challenged middle-American morality.

Perkins also deftly handled the touchy issues of censorship and libel, politely and deferentially asking Hemingway to modify unflattering allusions to living people in *The Torrents of Spring* and *The Sun Also Rises* and to find acceptable synonyms for objectionable vocabulary (a reference to bull 'balls' was changed to 'horns' in the published novel).[8] Perkins was looking out for Hemingway's and the press's mutual interests and wished to avoid the sort of problems that had interfered with the publication of James Joyce's *Ulysses*. Publishers could be held legally accountable for any obscene material they brought out, and Perkins likely knew that Boni & Liveright had balked at publishing *Ulysses* after Jane Heap and Margaret Anderson had each been fined for the serialization of excerpts in *The Little Review* in 1920. Perkins realized, too, that Hemingway expected Scribner to take risks with him that Liveright would not. Publishing material that the courts were likely to rule obscene was in neither the publisher's nor in Hemingway's best interest, but in his letters to Hemingway the editor was careful to frame his requests with unequivocal praise for the author's work and the genuine desire to see it brought to a wide market.

Scribner's gave Hemingway the wide audience that he wanted, but, more importantly, it gave him freedom to experiment with genre and form. As much as Hemingway's style is open to parody and imitation, none of his books is actually very much like any other, and he was constantly innovating – with mixed success. As Hemingway explained to Perkins, 'You see I would like, if you wanted, to write books for Scribner's to publish, for many years and would like them to be good books – better all the time – sometimes they might not be so good – but as well as I could write and perhaps with luck learning to write better all the time.'[9]

Hemingway knew himself to be a risky commodity to a publisher who wanted every book to be a best-seller. If Boni & Liveright had focused too much on cultivating Hemingway's highbrow credibility and not enough on his marketability, other publishers might err in the other direction. However, Hemingway was a perfect fit for the growing market of middlebrow, aspirational readers that Perkins and *Scribner's Magazine* editor Robert Bridges were courting, a readership who were now eager to read 'the moderns'. The middlebrow, and modernism itself, emerged in the first half of the twentieth century, products of a growing consumer culture conditioned to recognize and respond to branding, and they are best understood in operational terms rather than by any formal set of aesthetic criteria. Middlebrow modernism was both the works themselves and the know-how required to read them.[10] The partitioning of highbrow works from works with general appeal that had distinguished the lists of Boni & Liveright in the past no longer worked in a market that was rebranding 'highbrow' as 'literature of quality' and inviting mass-market readers to buy in.[11] Hemingway's work exemplified the balance between high art and mass appeal, and, as he later explained to Perkins, any short story collection needs accessible, plot-driven material too because it 'gives [readers] the necessary confidence in the stories that are hard for them'.[12]

Hemingway proved an attractive spokesmodel for modernism, an authentic yet accessible Paris bohemian with a handsome face that the marketing department readily placed on the dust jacket and advertisements for *The Sun Also Rises*.[13] Though he would loudly protest the use (and fabrication) by Scribner's of his life story as a marketing ploy, he nevertheless began to cultivate a distinct public image early on. As Matthew J. Bruccoli notes, 'Hemingway's best-invented fictional character was Ernest Hemingway.'[14] Hemingway wore many hats, but his best-known identity – Papa – was already taking shape as early as 1925.

'Papa' was an interesting moniker for a man who had ultimately failed to win his father's approval and whose future relationships with his own sons would be troubled. With an air of worldliness that belied his boyish face, Hemingway worked to become an expert in any arena that interested him and then, with paternalistic authority, dispensed his knowledge to those he deemed worthy of receiving what he called 'the true gen'. In his fiction, the heroes, too, possess this kind of insider knowledge – Jake Barnes, aficionado of the bullfight, is among the first, but others would follow: Robert Jordan and Santiago, of course, but also Catherine Barkley and Pilar, and the doomed Macombers (Francis Macomber will die before he ever gets to enjoy his newfound expertise). Hemingway found an attentive audience even in those older than himself. For example, Archibald MacLeish, who was seven years Hemingway's senior and a prolific writer who published a new volume of poetry yearly during his initial Paris tenure, addressed Hemingway as 'Pappy' in correspondence and conversation. Pauline, too, called him 'Papa', even before they started a family together, and *A Farewell to Arms* wasn't yet published before Hemingway began scolding Fitzgerald for his delay in finishing a novel to follow *Gatsby*.[15]

Part of this Papa persona depended upon his having a wife at his side, and Hemingway's marriage to Pauline followed his divorce from Hadley as rapidly as the Catholic Church and French bureaucracy allowed. In May 1927 Ernest and Pauline were married in both civil and Catholic ceremonies and embarked on a quiet honeymoon in Le Grau-du-Roi, a fishing village on the Mediterranean coast that had become a tourist destination. There he finished 'Hills Like White Elephants', a story in which a man and woman argue over whether or not to abort the pregnancy that has interrupted the 'fine time' they have been having as American expatriates in Europe who 'look at things and try new drinks'.[16] The subject matter seems incongruous with its timing; did this story of a lover's quarrel indicate that Hemingway's second marriage was already in trouble?

In fact, quite the opposite was true, and Hemingway's dedication of the manuscript to his new wife ('Mss for Pauline – Well, well well') prompts us to consider an alternative interpretation of the story, one that takes into account Hemingway's despair during the couple's enforced separation and the happy ending of their reunion.[17] In a letter written during the 100 days' separation, with Hemingway unsure whether Pauline would choose to return to him, he used both surgery and abortion as deliberately chosen metaphors for pain and separation. Perhaps Pauline, who had surely read and reread those letters and could recall them all by heart, would thus have understood the story very differently from the way Hemingway's readers saw it. In knowing how her own story concluded – choosing life with Ernest, she chose against the 'abortion' – Pauline may have readily seen a possibility that emerged for critics only decades later: the girl and man reach an agreement not to abort, and the girl does, in fact, 'feel fine' by story's end. When interpreted in this way, the unlikely honeymoon fiction becomes a testament to the wholeness and vitality of the Hemingway union.[18] It also demonstrates Hemingway's mastery of his craft: though Pauline may have understood the story one way, it nevertheless offers countless other possibilities for interpretation – not because the author lost control of his fiction or left out too much, but because he built ambivalence and ambiguity into the story so that, whichever ending the reader chooses, the story holds tightly together. In this sense, the story represents a significant improvement in Hemingway's skill, succeeding where earlier attempts at 'leave-out', like 'Out of Season', had fallen short. 'Hills Like White Elephants' was one of the 'hard' stories that could trouble the common reader – the kind of stories that he loved best.[19]

Men Without Women, which included 'Hills Like White Elephants', was well reviewed. Dorothy Parker called it 'magnificent' but sold Hemingway short by calling his talent 'reportorial' and his 'genius' 'an unerring sense of selection'.[20] Hemingway would always be annoyed by reviewers who assumed he had invented nothing and reported everything. Virginia Woolf regretted that the collection failed to 'go as deep or to promise as much' as a novel.[21] As he had done after the publication of In Our Time, Hemingway knew his next book needed to be a novel, but no novel was forthcoming, and his newfound fame only made the process more difficult. Before, when he had been working on his earliest fiction and was known only to locals and to other expatriate writers and artists in the Latin Quarter, he could move about Paris as he pleased, even writing in a neighbourhood café that was 'warm and clean and friendly'.[22]

Following the publication of *The Sun Also Rises*, however, the festival at Pamplona and Hemingway's Paris haunts had become tourist attractions, and Hemingway had to find new inspiration and new routines. Hemingway's friend, journalist Guy Hickok, poked fun at the unfounded gossip of tourists lurking around the Quarter trying to catch a glimpse of the artist at work:

> [Hemingway] is supposed to be kept up in Montmartre, drunk, in some back room where he writes priceless pages that fall on the floor and are taken out and sold by the people who keep him drunk.[23]

This image of Hemingway that conflated him with his characters was, Hickok insisted, nonsense – though it is one that has outlived its subject. The literary tourists did not seem to realize that the English spoken in the old cafés came from gawkers like themselves and not from the expatriates they had come to see, many of whom had already fled.

Paris in 1922 had been a good place to work; Paris in 1928 – not so much. Adding to a long list of illness and injury that season, a falling shard of glass from a broken bathroom skylight sliced the accident-prone Hemingway on the forehead, requiring a tourniquet and nine stitches. That accident and other mishaps may have had something to do with Hemingway's inability to complete work on a 'modern *Tom Jones*', though the story had fundamental problems unrelated to its author's bloodshed.[24] The father and son in that story were trying to get to Europe, but they, and the plot, were going nowhere. More likely, the accident, if it affected Hemingway's work at all, was actually a stroke of luck that 'set him free'.[25] With a scar on his forehead to match those of the old war wounds on his legs, Hemingway left his picaresque behind and began working on the manuscript that would become *A Farewell to Arms*. It was both a war novel and a romance, the dissonance of its subject matter reflected

Portrait of Ernest Hemingway by Helen Breaker, 1928. His visible head wound was the result of a falling skylight, one of many mishaps the accident-prone but resilient author sustained in his life.

in the paratactic narration of Frederic Henry, the wounded American ambulance driver who ultimately deserts at the retreat from Caporetto and flees with his nurse Catherine to neutral Switzerland, where she dies following the delivery of a stillborn baby. As this second novel started to take shape in Hemingway's mind, the Paris apprenticeship was over, and he and Pauline left Paris to the French and to the tourists.

They crossed the Atlantic and, following the advice of Dos Passos, stayed in Key West, Florida, waiting for their new automobile, a present from Pauline's wealthy uncle, Gus.[26] Key West in 1928 was a depopulated fishing town, and Hemingway found he was able to write there. He enjoyed the fishing and the eclectic band of local 'Conchs' who, he reported happily to Perkins, had never heard of F. Scott Fitzgerald or himself.[27] Pauline, who had got pregnant on their honeymoon, had no wish to have her baby in rustic Key West, so when her due date approached, Hemingway reluctantly moved on, first to Piggott, Arkansas, to stay with Pauline's parents, and then to Kansas City, Missouri, where Pauline could receive adequate obstetrical care. There she delivered their son via Caesarean section; the labour was hard on her, and, as Hemingway gruesomely put it in a letter to a friend, the doctor 'had to open Pauline up like a picador's horse'.[28]

In his nearly finished novel, Hemingway's heroine Catherine Barkley, too, would undergo a Caesarian section, but whereas Catherine and her baby died in the ordeal, Pauline and 4-kg (9-lb) Patrick were alive and well, apart from the difficult recovery typical of the surgery and the admonition from the doctor that she not become pregnant again soon. Hemingway had been an attentive parent to newborn Bumby, and he and Hadley had adjusted their routine and travels around the necessity of her breastfeeding the baby, but Hemingway appears to have been less invested in the early upbringing of his second son, departing only a month after the birth for Wyoming to fish and to finish his novel.[29] Neither was Pauline particularly maternal, delegating the care and feeding of the child to her sister Jinny. She wrote to her husband that motherhood was 'not very gripping' and that she looked forward to focusing her energies on being a wife.[30] As soon as she had recovered from her surgery, she left two-month-old Patrick with his aunt and grandmother and joined Hemingway in Wyoming. Though the death of Catherine Barkley and her baby must be read as the tragic victory of the natural world, it also hints towards the latent daydreams of an ambivalent husband and father: as Frederic walks alone into the rain, part of Hemingway may have begrudged him his freedom.

The reductive stance (albeit a necessary one in its own critical moment) that in Hemingway 'the only good woman is a dead one, and even then there are questions' has been widely discredited, but a kernel of truth remains.[31] Catherine cannot live, but being good does nothing either to hasten or to postpone her death. Death is universal and indiscriminate, and Frederic finds no comfort in imagining that the difficult labour is 'just nature giving her hell' because nature, as much as he might wish to personify it, has no feelings and no motives.[32] Death is wholly one-sided, like Frederic's unanswered prayers, and Frederic already knows this truth: 'That was what you did. You died. . . . You could count on that. Stay around and they would kill you.'[33] In lines Hemingway eventually cut from the novel, he rejects the idea that 'those who love things that are immortal and believe in them are immortal themselves', claiming that this notion is 'probably . . . not true. All that we can be sure of is that we are born and that we will die and that everything we love that has life will die too.'[34]

Catherine's death is less about any latent misogyny on Hemingway's part than it is Hemingway's take on the post-war world. The war had been for nothing in the end, just another way of dying: 'I had seen nothing sacred, and the things that were glorious had no glory and the sacrifices were like the stockyards at Chicago if nothing was done with the meat except to bury it.'[35] Even as this theme was well established early in the novel – Catherine's fellow nurse Helen Ferguson (Fergy) tells Frederic that their relationship is doomed: 'Fight or die. That's what people do. They don't marry' – Hemingway nevertheless had some trouble bringing the novel to a close.[36] It seemed clear that Catherine must die in childbirth, but what then?

Hemingway does not appear to have struggled in the initial composition of the novel. Cheerfully updating Perkins and other correspondents on the work in progress, he wrote page after page, drawing from his memories of his own war experience, primary and secondary sources about Italy and the First World War, and – to a far greater degree than his earliest critics and fans realized – his imagination. Revising the previous days' work as he went along, he finished the novel while travelling through the American West and set it aside for a while before attempting any further revisions.

Hemingway's brief respite was interrupted by the news that his father had died. Clarence, suffering from diabetes and despondent over worsening finances, had shot himself. When Hemingway got the news, he was on a train en route to Key West. He wired Fitzgerald for money, paid a Pullman porter to see five-year-old Bumby to his Florida destination, and reboarded a separate train for Illinois. There he learned the extent of his parents' financial problems and made a promise to his mother – which he kept – to keep her afloat and to pay for the younger siblings' educations.[37]

When he had arranged matters in Oak Park so that Grace and the youngest children could continue to live independently, he returned to Key West and to his novel, which his visiting sister Sunny had set to work typing. Hemingway convinced city slicker Perkins to pick up the book in person and come fishing. Max enjoyed the trip, not least because he knew the firm had landed another success.

Stylistically, the novel was quite different from what Hemingway had done in *In Our Time* and *The Sun Also Rises*. Critic Malcolm Cowley praised what he viewed as a newfound sophistication in the prose:

> the rhythm is more definite, the sentences are often longer, and the paragraphs are more carefully constructed. . . . [Hemingway] has added landscapes and interior monologues to his range of effects, and he has even begun to discuss ideas.

Whereas *The Sun Also Rises* had been an 'extended episode', *A Farewell to Arms* was, unquestionably, a novel.[38] Indeed, it would be *the* novel of the First World War in English in the way that Erich Maria Remarque's *All Quiet on the Western Front* (*Im Western Nichts Neues*), also published in 1929, would provide the German viewpoint of a war that had been, for both sides, devastating, confusing and stagnating.

Though Perkins had the typescript in hand, and the serialization of the novel in *Scribner's Magazine* – for which Hemingway earned $16,000 – was already under way, Hemingway still had two major problems to confront: first, he had to settle on an ending, and, second, he had to appease the editors at Scribner's who balked at his use of profanity.[39]

The first instalment had already appeared in the issue of *Scribner's Magazine* of May 1929 by the time Fitzgerald saw the manuscript, and he wrote Hemingway a letter with a number of suggested revisions. Fitzgerald felt that as the novel progressed, Hemingway left the war too far behind the scenes. He also recommended for deletion a number of scenes that Hemingway chose to retain.[40] Fitzgerald's suggestion to lop off the first few pages of *The Sun Also Rises* had greatly improved the beginning of that book, but Hemingway was understandably reluctant to allow Fitzgerald to serve as midwife on this novel as well – the debt would be too great. At the end of Fitzgerald's letter containing the unsolicited advice, Hemingway wrote simply, 'Kiss my ass EH.'[41] Hemingway would later declare in *The Paris Review* that he rewrote the last page of *A Farewell to Arms* 39 times, and this claim is hardly an exaggeration.[42] In his study of the novel's composition, Michael Reynolds counts at least 35 variant endings, including one in which the baby lives.[43] Hemingway even gave Fitzgerald's suggestion a try, moving the passage about how the world kills the brave from its location in Chapter 34 to the end, but that did not work either.[44] Finally, Hemingway settled on an ending and sent his protagonist 'back to the hotel in the rain'.[45]

The novel finally complete, Hemingway still had to contend with the nitpicky issues of censorship. Hemingway was not pleased with the publisher's objections to his vocabulary, changes that he wrote to Perkins would be an 'emasculation' of the book.[46] As Hemingway went over the proofs, he deferred to convention when it came to editing his punctuation but resisted substantive revisions, arguing that the obscene words appeared in both Shakespeare and Remarque.[47] Words like 'balls', 'fucking' and 'cocksucker' are, Hemingway explained, a constant presence in the language of soldiers, and he had used them sparingly, just to give the reader a hint of the world his characters inhabit. He urged Perkins to include as much as he could get away with. As Hemingway explained, he aimed not to degrade literature but to bring about 'the full use of the language', an accomplishment that 'may be of more value in the end than anything I write'.[48] Indeed, Hemingway's influence has been far-reaching, and is visible in much American war writing. Ultimately, however, Hemingway failed to get his way. The editors at Scribner's conceded some points, allowing him to retain 'bedpan', a term that was merely scatological and not sexual, but much of the profanity was represented by dashes. Even with the objectionable vocabulary obscured, the novel attracted the attention of the Boston police chief, who banned the issue of *Scribner's Magazine* that contained the second instalment of the serialization. The publicity may have actually boosted eventual sales of the novel, but the threat of legal action gave Perkins the clout he needed to convince Hemingway of the necessity of toning down the book's colourful language, and it was this sanitized version that was published on 27 September 1929.[49]

In its fall catalogue, Scribner's addressed, implicitly, the critics who had accused *The Sun Also Rises* of being shallow in its themes and subject matter. This sophomore attempt 'throws a far greater shadow than did the first. Its range is much wider, its implications more numerous, its significance more profound.'[50] Readers and reviewers agreed. The first edition of the book went through seven printings, totalling 101,675 copies, and was successful enough that Hemingway was able to renegotiate the terms of his contract to increase his royalty earnings.[51] Fanny Butcher, who had previously lauded Hemingway as a stylist but criticized his subject matter, praised the new novel without qualification. She deemed it the 'most interesting novel of the year' and Hemingway 'a most unusual genius of our day', but her assessment of Hemingway as 'the direct blossoming of Gertrude Stein's art' no doubt infuriated Hemingway.[52] More to Hemingway's liking, perhaps, was Malcolm Cowley's review, which recognized Hemingway as an already 'legendary figure', comparable in stature and influence to Joyce and Stendhal. Cowley suggested the possibility that '"A Farewell to Arms" is a symbolic title . . . Hemingway's farewell to a period, an attitude, and perhaps to a method also', and indeed it was.[53] With the critical and commercial success of the novel, Hemingway could now leave the remnants of his bohemian identity behind.

Hemingway said his goodbyes and all but turned out the lights on the City of Light. In his introduction from 1929 to the memoirs of famed artists' model Kiki, Hemingway declared the 'era of Montparnasse' to be 'definitely marked as closed', and good riddance: 'personally I don't think it was worth much.'[54] Likewise, with the poem 'Valentine', published in the issue of the *Little Review* of May 1929, Hemingway bid farewell, too, to the little magazines in which he had begun his career. Hemingway's poems had served as writing exercises for his apprentice fiction and as a quick and easy way to get his name into the little magazines of expatriate Paris; now that he had mastered both the short story and the novel – becoming famous in the process – this sarcastic little love note was the last poem Hemingway would ever be compelled to publish in a little magazine.[55] His talent and fame now outshone that of his former mentors. He was a man of letters and a celebrity, and the reading public eagerly awaited his next novel. It would be a long wait.

6

Shootism versus Sport, 1929–35

Archibald MacLeish would write of Hemingway in an elegiac poem about Paris in the 1920s, ' . . . Fame became of him / Veteran out of the wars before he was twenty: / Famous at twenty-five: thirty a master –'.[1] With each subsequent book, Hemingway's sun had risen higher. Only 27 years old when *The Sun Also Rises* was published, Hemingway experienced a sort of celebrity heretofore unheard of for any American author excepting Mark Twain and, perhaps, his contemporary and rival F. Scott Fitzgerald.

With *A Farewell to Arms*, Hemingway had managed to write an anti-war novel that was at heart a love story (or a love story that was at heart an anti-war novel). Perhaps he could have pounded out a few more novels like *A Farewell to Arms* – guaranteed best-sellers and *Cosmopolitan* serials that mixed love and war. However, he kept the big picture of his career in mind and was wary of his early acclaim. Following the success of the novels *The Sun Also Rises* and *A Farewell to Arms* and of his short story collection *Men Without Women*, Hemingway was cautious about relying on previous formulas. He had no intention of being one of the young novelists who 'write one interesting novel . . . then to be followed by other novels, demanded by the success of the first . . . and all the time the author never living any life or learning anything or seeing anything.'[2] Though readers eagerly anticipated another novel, his next major project would finally see his attempting the bullfighting book alluded to in his early correspondence with Perkins.

In 1930 Hemingway began working on the bullfighting compendium *Death in the Afternoon*. It defied the expectations of his publisher and his readers, broke generic convention and blurred the lines between fiction and non-fiction. Hemingway's original conclusion to *Death in the Afternoon* addresses his own refusal to turn out another best-selling novel, noting that giving in to financial incentives and the expectations of the reading public would mean compromising his artistic integrity.[3] This section of the book was ultimately cut, but his decision to let the book make its own way in the market, unassisted by serialization in *Scribner's Magazine* or adoption by the Book of the Month Club – which would have increased sales and exposure but necessitated cuts and self-censorship – demonstrates his commitment to these principles.

A reader wishing to gain an introduction to the rules and history of the spectacle of the bullfight could certainly find much to learn in its pages; terms are defined, and the division of labour between picadors, banderilleros and matador is explained. Hemingway's explanations of the bullfight offer, too, an ethnography of Spain, suggesting that the Spanish identity is as varied as its geography. Practices and traditions vary from town to town, with Madrid being 'the most Spanish of all cities', even as it outwardly appears the most modern.[4] Hemingway would, later in the decade, return to Madrid to report on the Spanish Civil War and to argue in print for the Republican cause. Anyone who wonders why Hemingway maintained such passionate loyalty to the Spanish people, or who suggests that he used the war as an excuse to shirk his domestic responsibilities, need only look at *Death in the Afternoon* to find the source of his deep connection to the place. Hemingway found in Spain an escape from modernity.[5] To Hemingway, Spain felt immediately familiar and right – a landscape that recalled the backdrop of his favourite childhood memories in the Michigan woods, even as it offered the ancient and strange rituals of the bullfight and the various Catholic feasts alongside a pre-war idealism that had been lost in Italy, France and the United States. A self-proclaimed aficionado and Catholic convert, Hemingway had managed to infiltrate a culture that was not his own, and with *Death in the Afternoon*, he took on the challenge of presenting that culture to his readers so that they might understand it at a higher level beyond that which they might achieve on their own, even if they themselves travelled to Spain, Baedeker travel guide in hand. As an ethnography, however, the project was not entirely successful, with Hemingway playing contradictory roles of tourist (outsider), aficionado (insider) and translator (mediator).[6] As extensive as Hemingway's reading on Spain and the bullfight was, and as passionately and intuitively as he absorbed its rituals, he remained an outsider whose fascination was captured by the exhilarating strangeness of the all-important first encounter and the subsequent excitement at insinuating himself into a subculture that metonymically represented Spain itself. The adoption of a self-consciously parochial understanding of the bullfighting practice – which differed significantly from village to village and even ranch to ranch – was thus ultimate cosmopolitan turn as Hemingway presented himself as a well-travelled citizen of the world.

The practice of bullfighting may have changed over time, modernizing to accommodate improved technology and to mitigate concerns about animal rights, but *Death in the Afternoon* remains relevant as Hemingway's *ars poetica*, even as its usefulness as a practical guide to bullfighting has expired. Hemingway argues that when the action of a book is 'stated . . . purely enough' the work 'would be as valid in a year or in ten years or, with luck . . . always'.[7] But as Hemingway's metacommentary suggests, 'It's very hard to write like this', and *Death in the Afternoon*, with its digressions, allusions and reflections on the bravery of the animals and artistry of the toreadors, provides insight not only into how the bullfight functions as a theme and as a metaphor throughout the author's body of work, but into the craft of writing itself.[8] The 'science' of the book is not one of tauromachy but of literary criticism – and sly literary criticism at that.[9] Throughout much of the book, Hemingway turns from the discussion of the bullfight to give insight into his philosophy of writing and art, often in the form of dialogue with an interlocutor known as the 'Old lady'. Full of quotable (and, subsequently, oft-quoted) platitudes about writing delivered in conversation with this old lady, the book is a dialogue with Gertrude Stein – and thus with modernism itself. The fate of the old lady, then, is telling: 'We threw her out of the book, finally,' the author tells us, right before moving into the section of the book offering the most sustained commentary about the craft of writing.[10]

> When writing a novel a writer should create living people; people not characters. A *character* is a caricature. If a writer can make people live there may be no great characters in his book, but it is possible that his book will remain as a whole.[11]

This advice echoes the metafictional opening of Fitzgerald's story 'The Rich Boy', which had been published in 1926: 'Begin with an individual, and before you know it you find that you have created a type; begin with a type, and you find that you have created – nothing.'[12] Hemingway's advice goes further, needling a bit, perhaps, at Fitzgerald's prodigious talent for turning out exquisitely wrought sentences in even the most commercial fiction:

> No matter how good a phrase or a simile [the writer] may have if he puts it in where it is not absolutely necessary and irreplaceable he is spoiling his work for egotism. Prose is architecture, not interior decoration, and the Baroque is over.[13]

The passage is also directed towards author-critics, and at Aldous Huxley, who had criticized Hemingway's work, in particular, with Hemingway positioning himself as a man of action: the critic performs while the writer writes.[14] Crucial, too, is that the writer avoids abstraction. In its most famous passage, the book lays out Hemingway's 'iceberg' theory of writing:

> If a writer of prose knows enough about what he is writing about he may omit things that he knows and the reader, if the writer is writing truly enough, will have a feeling of those things as strongly as though the writer had stated them. The dignity of movement of an ice-berg is due to only one-eighth of it being above water.[15]

Into the book should go the sum total of the writer's experience, and, taking his own advice, Hemingway worked on *Death in the Afternoon* for three years. His work was disrupted for five months following a car crash and badly broken arm, and once he had recovered the physical ability to write, he still struggled to put everything he knew of Spain into the work. The Hemingways returned to Spain for another bullfighting season, and Hemingway set about gathering photographs for the book.

In the same season that Hemingway brought *Death in the Afternoon* to its conclusion, Pauline gave birth to their son Gregory Hancock Hemingway, and the family settled down in Key West. Disappointed that the child was not the daughter he and Pauline had hoped for, Hemingway paid even less attention to this baby than he had to Patrick; Patrick, jealous of his little brother, doused the infant in insecticide.[16] Meanwhile, Pauline's doctor warned her not to become pregnant again, as her uterus could not bear the ordeal a third time. The doctor's admonition, coupled with Pauline's adherence to Catholic doctrine prohibiting the use of birth control, may have put a damper on the Hemingways' conjugal relationship. Nevertheless, the Hemingways' home life remained relatively stable during this time, and the family purchased an elegant two-storey house on Whitehead Street in Key West. The house, paid for by

Pauline's wealthy Uncle Gus, was a gift from the childless uncle who indulged his niece and sought the favour of her talented husband. Gus had also purchased the Hemingways' car, and he was eager to finance Ernest Hemingway's long-awaited African safari, though the author's injuries and the necessity of finishing *Death in the Afternoon* had postponed plans for that trip.[17]

In an introduction to the edition of *In Our Time* published by Scribner's in 1930, the noted literary critic Edmund Wilson had observed how the stories and vignettes contain, on a smaller scale, much of what makes Hemingway's 'more ambitious books' distinctive: 'Candor and cold-bloodedness both belong to the same humanity' in Hemingway's work, Wilson writes, and though much of life is 'enjoyable', 'the brutality of life is always there, and it is somehow bound up with the enjoyment.'[18] Despite Wilson's assessment of a mid-career Hemingway, which anticipates the themes of *Death in the Afternoon* as much as it describes *The Sun Also Rises* and *A Farewell to Arms*, when *Death in the Afternoon* appeared readers ultimately resisted the unfamiliar material about bullfighting.

Death in the Afternoon was published in September 1932, and, as Scribner's had predicted (and Hemingway had refused to believe), the book did not sell well. Appearing when the nation was mired in the Great Depression, the book was unaccountably immense and included 81 photographs. From the beginning, it faced an uphill battle: the Scribner's advertising department was not sure how or to whom to market this unclassifiable tome, and Hemingway resisted advertising it as anything other than a book on bullfighting – even though it very much was one.[19] One thing reviewers and readers could agree upon, however, was that the book was different from anything Hemingway had done before.

H. L. Mencken proclaimed the book 'an extraordinarily fine piece of expository writing' that, unfortunately, 'often descends to a gross and irritating cheapness' and suggested that Hemingway had gone to great lengths 'to prove fatuously that he is a naughty fellow'.[20]

Other reviewers took a similar stance. Hemingway had little patience for Mencken, to whom he had facetiously dedicated *The Torrents of Spring*, but it was to Robert Coates, whose negative review of *Death in the Afternoon* appeared in the *New Yorker*, that Hemingway wrote a public reply. His response, on 5 November 1932, denies Coates's assessment that the book had been unnecessarily critical of other authors and implies that Coates lacks a sense of humour: 'There are no subjects that I would not jest about if the jest was funny enough (just as, liking wing shooting, I would shoot my own mother if she went in coveys and had a good strong flight).'[21]

The review that generated the angriest response, however, was undoubtedly that of the radical critic Max Eastman. In the *New Republic* in June 1933, Eastman wrote that *Death in the Afternoon* contains 'an unconscionable quantity of bull' made up of 'juvenile romantic gushing and sentimentalizing of simple facts'. Striking at the very heart of the Hemingway ethos – which insisted on truths pared down to their most basic elements – the review goes so far as to suggest Hemingway's take on the bullfight is nothing more than 'fairy-story writing' and 'sentimental poppycock'. Worse yet, Eastman accuses Hemingway of having spawned a 'literary style . . . of wearing false hair on the chest'.[22] Hemingway, taking the remark literally, was insulted as much for the perceived slight to his manhood as for the criticism of his work, and he seethed in letters to Perkins and others that he intended to avenge himself if the opportunity ever arose.[23] He wasn't kidding. Hemingway was capable of holding lifelong grudges, and when he ran into Eastman in Perkins's office four years later, his anger boiled over and he smacked Eastman in the face with a copy of the critic's collected work – which included the offending review. The incident made the papers, though accounts of the altercation vary.[24] Whether Hemingway allowed Eastman to pin him to the floor or if Eastman won the fight remains a matter of conjecture, but the public's interest in the incident demonstrates Hemingway's celebrity. He was in the news not because of any recent literary achievement but simply for being Hemingway, with a public persona treading a little too closely to caricature. *Vanity Fair*, which in 1924 had rejected a humorous piece by him about bullfighting, now glibly included in its pages a Hemingway paper doll by illustrator Constantin Alajálov which billed the 'hard-drinking, hard-fighting, and hard-loving' author as 'America's own literary cave man'.[25] The doll, clothed in animal skins, could be further outfitted as café denizen, fisherman, wounded soldier or toreador.

This celebrity did not, however, guarantee that people would buy his books, and his latest short story collection, *Winner Take Nothing* (1933), languished. The first printing of 20,300 copies did not sell out, and royalties earned would not even have covered the $6,000 advance Hemingway had taken on the book; the publisher's records indicate that six years later, 2,000 copies would be remaindered.[26] The book's relative failure was the result of a number of factors, not all of them the fault of Scribner's marketing department or the stagnant economy. For his part, Hemingway had produced little new fiction in the years since *A Farewell to Arms* and had disappointed readers with *Death in the Afternoon*, so the initial audience was not what it might have been even a few years earlier. There seems to have been little word-of-mouth publicity for the book as sales dropped off precipitously in the weeks following its debut, despite its release in time for the Christmas shopping season. As the title suggests, the subject matter was not particularly uplifting and included a botched castration attempt, shell shock, syphilis and suicide. Even Hemingway himself knew that the stories were 'mostly about things and people that people won't care about – or will actively dislike', but they were, too, his attempt to write 'a picture of the whole world'.[27]

Underappreciated in their time, some of the stories in the collection have had lasting importance in the Hemingway canon, contributing to reassessments of his work that consider

Hemingway's portrayal of gender and sexuality. 'The Sea Change', for example, in which a female protagonist breaks up with her boyfriend to pursue a lesbian relationship, challenges the view that Hemingway's work is exclusively heteronormative or masculinist. Far from being an exception, 'The Sea Change' insists that readers and critics revisit Hemingway's portrayal of gender and sexuality in 'Mr and Mrs Elliot', *The Sun Also Rises* and many, if not all, of the Nick Adams stories.[28] Indeed, it provides further evidence to secure Hemingway's place as a modernist writer (and not just a writer working in the modernist period).

'A Clean, Well-Lighted Place' is another story in the collection that evinces the complexity of Hemingway's work. The story is quintessential Hemingway: two waiters in a Spanish café argue about women and suicide as an old man drinks heavily and then goes off, alone, into the night. The original version of the story, as it appeared in *Scribner's Magazine* and *Winner Take Nothing*, is deeply perplexing. Subsequent editions, published posthumously, have erroneously emended the text in a botched attempt to smooth out an interpretive crux in the waiters' dialogue. In its unaltered form, the story, which Hemingway reportedly claimed 'tops them all for leave-out', poses existential questions and adamantly refuses the reader any answers.[29] Readers who may have expected clarity and directness from Hemingway's pared-down style received, instead, modernist experimentation with intersubjectivity that more closely resembles Joycean stream-of-consciousness. Indeed, Joyce called the story 'one of the best short stories ever written'.[30]

Even as Hemingway's work firmly situated him among the most important writers of his day, the author himself, in then-remote Key West, could retreat from the larger world, with its highbrow literary circles, and surround himself with people who were indifferent to his other life as a famous author. On the blue water, Hemingway had found a new diversion – marlin fishing – and this pastime, more than the new baby or the new house, bound him to Key West. As he did with anything that interested him, Hemingway worked to learn all he could about the Gulf Stream and billfish, reading widely on the subject and seeking the expertise of locals who had made a living fishing for marlin long before American sportsmen 'discovered' the practice. He learned quickly, and soon was setting records and assisting researchers in the classification of Atlantic species. Unlike the bullfight, the origins of which can be traced to prehistoric times, deep-sea fishing, as a sport, was something new and modern, and Hemingway was among its first practitioners. Indeed, he helped to popularize Gulf fishing much as *The Sun Also Rises* had brought hordes of tourists to Pamplona.[31]

His newfound knowledge worked its way into his fiction as well, as in a passage in *To Have and Have Not* (1937) that draws upon Hemingway's fishing log of 1933.[32] This expertise would also, much later, be put to use in *The Old Man and the Sea* (1952). Big-game fishing in the Gulf Stream was more than just a hobby: it would 'invigorate his mature work' in much the same way that 'trout fishing in a postindustrial landscape' had influenced 'the emergent Hemingway'.[33] His move to big-game fishing in the summer of 1933 parallels the move in his work to take on greater subject matter in larger books. In the Gulf Stream, both Hemingway the angler and Hemingway the author found 'the last wild country there is left', and he was eager to explore it.[34]

Hemingway was also eager to fulfil a lifelong dream of going on safari. Unfortunately, readers and critics who had resisted Hemingway's first non-fiction tome proved even less receptive when the author, who had not produced a novel since *A Farewell to Arms*, turned his sights to Africa. The travails of the celebrity author's *mano a mano* competition to claim the largest trophies were irrelevant to readers in the United States, where crops and banks were failing and unemployment was on the rise. Hemingway defended the scope and expense of the trip as being a crucial part of his job – if he didn't travel and hunt and fish he would have

Hemingway poses with the horns of kudu and oryx on safari in Africa, 1934.

nothing to write about – but Americans in the midst of the deepening Depression were hardly the audience for such a book.[35]

The Hemingways departed in August 1933 and spent two months in Europe before setting out for Africa. They were joined in France by Charles Thompson, Hemingway's Key West fishing buddy. Meanwhile, the children had been placed with separate caregivers.[36] From Marseilles, the party sailed to Port Said, Egypt, passed through the Suez Canal and disembarked in Mombasa, where they caught a train to Nairobi and, from there, ventured into the countryside, where they could begin their hunt. They met up with Philip Percival, the 'white hunter' who had accompanied former president Theodore Roosevelt on his headline-making safari in 1909.[37] In Hemingway's Key West library, among other books on African hunting, was Roosevelt's account of that trip, *African Game Trails*, published by Scribner's.[38] Roosevelt had been one of Hemingway's boyhood heroes, and though Hemingway was a seasoned traveller and experienced hunter, the Africa trip was nevertheless a childhood dream come true.

Circumstances conspired to keep the adventure from being perfect, however. At one of the early stops along the way – Hemingway believed it to have been in Port Said – he contracted a case of amoebic dysentery. Despite suffering from extreme pain and alarming blood loss, Hemingway, undaunted, went out hunting as planned, but the illness eventually required his hospitalization in Nairobi. In the hospital, he was pumped full of the drug emetine, which, despite side effects only slightly less unpleasant than the dysentery, proved effective and he soon returned to the hunt with renewed energy.[39] The ensuing pursuit of a greater kudu trophy – the male of this distinctive antelope species being characteristically elusive and known for its unusual spiral-shaped horns – fuelled this last stage of the adventure and captured Hemingway's imagination.

Hemingway's experiment in the resulting book-length account of the trip, *Green Hills of Africa*, published on 25 October 1935, was doomed to fail, and not simply because the Depression-era market was in no mood for such a book. Hemingway was exploring in theory and in practice a philosophy on writing that, if successful, would go wholly overlooked by the general reader. He explains in an *Esquire* letter from October 1935:

> The more [a writer] learns from experience the more truly he can imagine. If he gets so he can imagine truly enough people will think that the things he relates all really happened and that he is just reporting.

Having been a journalist before he was a published author, Hemingway understood the key difference: 'If it was reporting they would not remember it.' Topical news stories are, he explains, quickly forgotten. 'But if you make it up instead of describe it you can make it round and whole and solid and give it life.'[40] He had made up *A Farewell to Arms* so convincingly that many readers believed him to be a veteran of a battle that occurred when he was still in high school. In *Green Hills of Africa*, he tries to further articulate his philosophy of writing and to put the philosophy into practice with a story that blurs the line between novel and memoir. The result was not entirely successful, at least not in a way that his readers could comprehend.

In a passage almost catechism-like in its use of question and answer, Hemingway explains American literature to Kandisky, an Austrian the party met on the roadside and who had recognized him as the *Dichter* (poet) published a decade earlier in the German little magazine *Der Querschnitt*. Hemingway responds that the problem with writers like Nathaniel Hawthorne was that they did not realize that a classic cannot imitate the classics that have come before it. A new classic is unavoidably influenced by earlier works, but it must itself be a new kind of book, and writers must try to transcend the physics of the known world to achieve a 'fourth and fifth dimension', 'a prose that has never been written'.[41] The stated goal of *Green Hills of Africa* is to attempt this new form of expression; simultaneously *Künstlerroman*, safari memoir, catechism, novel, guidebook and manifesto, it self-reflexively challenges generic convention.

In describing the book to Perkins, Hemingway compared it to 'Big Two-Hearted River', calling it 'a landscape painting' with 'plenty of excitement', but once again sales of the book fell short of his expectations, and the promised excitement failed to materialize for the common reader.[42] The book was 'of several parts, any one of which was offensive to someone', an unanticipated result of the not-quite-successful experiment with 'multidimensional prose'.[43] A further problem was the book's timing. Not only was the book out of place among the populist fiction of the 1930s by John Steinbeck, Erskine Caldwell and, to some degree, William Faulkner, but, as a manifesto of modernism, it came too late. Hemingway was not the only Scribner's author struggling in the difficult market. The previous year, F. Scott Fitzgerald had finally brought out his follow-up novel to *The Great Gatsby*. *Tender Is the Night* (1934) is a sprawling account of one man's decline set against the backdrop of the French Riviera, but, as Malcolm Cowley noted, 'now that the ball is ending in tragedy, [Fitzgerald] doesn't know how to describe it.'[44] Meanwhile, Perkins had been hard at work helping Thomas Wolfe cut his sophomore novel, *Of Time and the River*, to a more manageable 900-odd pages. The editor was, understandably, anxiously awaiting Hemingway's next novel, and though he was not completely satisfied to get a safari memoir instead, his interactions with the writer were, as always, measured, conciliatory and patient. Hemingway, meanwhile, was in no rush to write a novel. While he had been hard at work bringing the safari to the page in four dimensions, he was also expanding his interest in deep-sea fishing. Hemingway realized that he needed a fishing vessel of his own, and in 1934 he bought a boat, which he christened *Pilar*, the name he and Pauline had intended for their baby should Gregory have been born a girl. This time he made the purchase himself, not with Uncle Gus's money, but with an advance for contributions to the new men's magazine *Esquire*.

Founded in 1933, *Esquire* was something different: a mainstream, middlebrow magazine for men, about men and produced with a distinctly masculinist sensibility. Though it contained its share of pin-up girl art – the iconic 'Vargas Girls' of the 1940s would originate in its pages – it was no pulp magazine. Its content was made up of articles on politics, sports, literature, fashion and travel geared towards a male, heterosexual audience that aspired to affluence. Editor-in-chief Arnold Gingrich's ideal audience consisted of 'ex-Babbitts', 'guys who never heard of' little magazines like *The Dial*, but who nevertheless could cultivate an appreciation for good writing.[45] Gingrich solicited material from a number of famous writers, including Caldwell, John Dos Passos and Dashiell

Hammett, but the fledgling magazine needed to include Hemingway's byline from the very first issue in order to define and endorse its purpose. From 1933 until 1936, Hemingway would contribute more than 25 pieces, billed as 'letters'. The letters, written from Cuba, Spain, Paris and even Africa, took readers along on the author's travels and provided advice on fishing, shooting and, of course, writing.

The new magazine's pose was at once literary and anti-literary, and no author better fitted that ethos than Ernest Hemingway. The relationship was reciprocal. The 'letters' helped to shape Hemingway's public persona, and when American men 'turned to *Esquire* in order to answer questions of style', they found in Hemingway's letters the particular brand of masculine cosmo-modernism that distinguished the 'traveler' from the 'tourist'.[46] From the Gulf Stream to Africa, Hemingway experienced the adventures that the world had to offer and wrote about them in the sagacious tones of his 'Papa' persona so that his readers could glean this insider knowledge from the comfort of their own armchairs. *Esquire* was a success, and the magazine moved quickly from a quarterly to a monthly, reaching hundreds of thousands of readers.

As he described the initial project to Hemingway, Gingrich somewhat presumptuously suggested that Hemingway reread part of *Death in the Afternoon* before writing on the subject of marlin fishing, in order to 'spill over' into the articles on Cuba and fishing 'something of . . . Spain and the bullfight'. Gingrich asked for 'the sights and sounds and sweats and odors – the whole rhythmic pattern – of this separate life that revolves about the central fact of the fight with the swordfish as that other does about the fight with the bull'.[47] In the first instalment of the series, 'Marlin off the Morro: A Cuban Letter' (1933), Hemingway delivers Gingrich's requested material, but traces are discernible, too, of the small boy who sought to add to the collection of his local Agassiz club. Hemingway suggests in this catalogue of the various kinds of fish swimming off the Cuban coast that 'anyone seeking notoriety for himself by naming new species could have a field day.'[48] Indeed, Hemingway invited aboard his vessel scientists, who studied the marlin he was able to haul out of the Gulf Stream waters, and they reclassified white and blue marlin as separate species.[49] In appreciation, the ichthyologist Henry W. Fowler named a newly classified fish after the author: *Neomerinthe hemingwayi*, or spinycheek scorpionfish, a small but suitably rugged fish.[50] Hemingway had his own thoughts about fish taxonomy but explains to *Esquire* readers that his stance is 'too complicated a theory to go into'. While his detractors have often accused Hemingway of posturing and braggadocio, Fowler's appreciative gesture indicates that his claim here is not merely a pose.

The practices of marlin fishing work, too, as a way of understanding Hemingway's literary experiments during this period. Carlos Gutierrez, Hemingway's angling mentor and first mate, taught Hemingway to place baits 64 metres (35 fathoms) deep and to drift in the current, waiting for something to strike – 'deep drifting meant confronting the unknown', and the approach often hauled up large fish not visible from the surface.[51] However, the fisherman who rigged baits in such depth also risked the false hope that the one that got away would have dwarfed any known specimens – 'every time a fish takes the bait drifting you have a feeling perhaps you are hooked to one of these', Hemingway wrote.[52] Eventually, however, Hemingway gave up drift fishing, arguing that prize specimens could also be caught nearer the surface, where the fisherman could see his prey.[53] *Death in the Afternoon* and *Green Hills of Africa* were new species, the result of a type of literary drift fishing, but they were not record-breakers. To land the biggest quarry, Hemingway needed to return to the surface and to the form of the novel. In the meantime, with the Depression ongoing at home and revolution in Spain – and war in Europe – imminent, a dormant social conscience was awakened, and Hemingway was ready for the challenge of new subject matter.

7

The Soul of Spain, 1935–9

Hemingway's detractors had occasionally accused him of lacking the social conscience that was the moral obligation of the serious artist. In an article titled 'The Dumb Ox', the avant-garde English painter and author Wyndham Lewis charged that 'it is difficult to imagine a writer whose mind is more entirely closed to politics than is Hemingway's.'[1] Lewis's own early support of Adolf Hitler – which he later recanted – lends some degree of retrospective dubiety to his opinion, but other prominent critics, too, such as Heywood Broun, Granville Hicks and Edmund Wilson, voiced similar criticisms. Such a characterization is not entirely unfounded, as Hemingway did avoid associating with any party line. He was 'apolitical or antipolitical', distrusting governments and political parties in general.[2] As Hemingway makes clear in *Death in the Afternoon*, didactic writing is bad writing; to write the kind of noble heroes that some critics expected of him would have been a betrayal of his craft. He was not, however, apathetic, and much of his work during the 1930s demonstrates his commitment to causes he believed in.

Though Hemingway was generally unscathed by the worsening conditions of the Great Depression, as a citizen of Key West he was witness to those who were not so fortunate. As one critic would aptly note, Hemingway's Key West, 'like the Paris of 1925' was both an 'outpost of a culture and its symbol'.[3] Hemingway, at once part of it and apart from it, was drawn to the noisy, shabby, deeply moving rancor and tumult of all those human wrecks, the fishermen and the Cuban revolutionaries, the veterans and the alcoholics, the gilt-edged snobs and the hungry natives, the great white stretch of beach promising everything and leading nowhere.[4]

Among the down-and-out populace of Key West was a group of First World War veterans sent down to the Florida Keys to work on federal road-building projects as part of Roosevelt's Civilian Conservation Corps. When 458 of the veterans perished in a hurricane, Hemingway, outraged, placed the blame squarely on the U.S. government. In a piece written for the *New Masses*, the ostensible, if not the official, publication of the Communist Party of America, Hemingway suggests that the veterans' presence in the Keys was a retaliation for the activities of the Bonus Army, a group of 15,000 First World War veterans who had congregated peacefully in front of the Capitol in 1932 seeking early payout of a promised veterans bonus. President Hoover called in an army regiment to force the demonstrators to abandon their shantytown, but many of them had nowhere else to go.[5] The decision to send the veterans down during hurricane season – a time when 'wealthy people, yachtsmen, fishermen such as President Hoover and President Roosevelt, do not come' – indicated to Hemingway the irresponsibility of those to whom 'veterans, especially the bonus-marching variety' had less value than the yachts that the wealthy arranged to be moved to safe harbours: 'the veterans had been sent there; they had no opportunity to leave, nor any protection against hurricanes; and they never had a chance for their lives'.[6]

Little was known at the time about what we now call post-traumatic stress disorder, but Hemingway was aware of the condition and of the government's irresponsibility in handling veterans who suffered from it. Sending veterans – 'many of them

Hemingway with his wife Pauline and his three sons, Jack, Patrick and Gregory, on the Bimini docks in the summer of 1936.

close to the border of pathological cases' – to the Keys during hurricane season was, Hemingway suggested, yet another way the veterans had been abandoned, if not outright murdered, by the u.s. government.[7] In the article, he returns to his journalistic roots and offers a gruesome eyewitness account of the aftermath of the hurricane that hit Matecumbe Key in 1935: men who had sought shelter behind the railroad embankment were now

> face down and face up in the mangroves . . . Then further
> on you found them high in the trees where the water swept
> them. You found them everywhere and in the sun all of
> them were beginning to be too big for their blue jeans and
> jackets that they could never fill when they were on the bum
> and hungry.[8]

The u.s. government was not Hemingway's only target. He also got some shots in at a certain type of risk-averse writer, the kind who safely experiences the hurricane from the Florida mainland in order to use the material in future work. In contrast, Hemingway himself (characteristically voiced as 'you') adeptly reads the storm chart and secures his own boat before the storm hits and afterwards goes, personally, into the mangroves to help retrieve the bodies. The article is, of course, as much about the author himself as it is a call to action. Even as he points a finger at the u.s. government, he draws a portrait of himself as knowledgeable, fearless and a friend to the common man, though not himself entirely one of them. Though he might be writing for the *New Masses*, he is one of the 'haves'. Straddling a space between the wealthy interlopers from the mainland and the workers, vets and other various have-nots, Hemingway derives his living from the physical and mental labour of his writerly art.

The Russian critic and translator Ivan Kashkin had written that Hemingway, 'a consummate literary craftsman' and 'perfect sportsman and globe trotter', needed to find a 'high purpose' in his work to take it to the next level, and Hemingway replied to Kashkin that the 'life of action' is all part of the 'perpetual challenge' of writing.[9] Hemingway, who did not normally take criticism well, responded in measured, thoughtful tones and explained:

> A writer is an outlyer . . . He can be class conscious only if his talent is limited. If he has enough talent all classes are his province. He takes from them all and what he gives is everybody's property . . . A true work of art endures forever; no matter what its politics.[10]

Hemingway existed both in the world and apart from it – a willing participant in all life had to offer but exempt, too, from any responsibility but the very personal artistic imperative of recording his experiences. He thus exempted himself from the responsibility to write proletarian fiction and from his own critique of the rich whose presence in the Keys is as ubiquitous as the storms that batter the islands yearly from August to October.

Though not a 'Conch' himself, Hemingway was an insider welcome among the Key West locals. Instead of being part of a literary scene as he had been in Paris – or even in his earliest days in Key West when fellow writers like John Dos Passos or Archibald MacLeish had joined him to go fishing – Hemingway now cultivated friendships with locals and with non-literary sporting types, a circumstance that Florida novelist Marjorie Kinnan Rawlings thought suggested an 'inner conflict between the sporting life and the literary life', a view that contradicts the arguments he had made to Kashkin and others that the sport fuelled the art.[11] In the second half of 1936, however, civil war in Spain brought him out of the comfortable microcosm that he had built around himself and put him back into a community of artists, writers, film-makers and revolutionaries. To Pauline's dismay, he would head into the fray himself, but it was not just the war that captured Hemingway's attention. He had fallen under the spell of a young writer from St Louis named Martha Gellhorn, whose fearlessness and beauty were matched by her talent and social conscience, and she, too, was anxious to get to Spain.

In December 1936, Gellhorn, wearing her signature little black dress, walked into Sloppy Joe's, where a distinctive 'large, dirty man' was drinking at the bar.[12] Though only 28 years old and accompanied by her mother and younger brother, Gellhorn was no ingénue. Hemingway would later model a character in his play *The Fifth Column* after her, giving the blonde journalist Dorothy Bridges 'the same background all American girls have that come to Europe with a certain amount of money', namely, 'college, money in family, now more or less than it was, usually less now, men, affairs, abortions, ambitions'.[13] Dorothy, like Martha, writes. Already Martha had lived abroad, been married and separated in practice if not by law, cultivated friendships with the writer H. G. Wells and First Lady Eleanor Roosevelt and published a novel, an ethnography and a collection of short stories. Hemingway's and Gellhorn's biographers have typically characterized this first encounter as a chance meeting, the result of Gellhorn's impromptu trip to Key West during a Miami vacation.[14] However, as Hemingway grouses in 'The Sights of Whitehead Street: A Key West Letter', his home was already well known as a tourist attraction, listed in Works Progress Administration tourist literature since at least 1934.[15] Gellhorn had used lines from *A Farewell to Arms* as the epigraph of her first novel, *What Mad Pursuit* (1934), and his name had also been invoked by way of favourable comparison in reviews of her book *The Trouble I've Seen* (1936).[16] Certainly she was well aware of the work and general whereabouts of the country's most famous author, and her Key West jaunt may have been the mad pursuit of an ambitious and headstrong writer out to apprentice herself to the most prominent literary talent of the day. Of course, their meeting may well have been luck – whether that luck was good or bad is a matter that Martha would later come to question.

In any event, the encounter in December 1936 at Sloppy Joe's was the beginning of a rapport between the two writers, one that may well have made Pauline immediately nervous. A decade after she herself had joined Ernest and Hadley in Schruns and at Juan-les-Pins, Pauline now found herself in the role of the wife whose husband has attracted the persistent attentions – carried out under the guise of friendship – of an attractive and exciting young woman. Martha's presence was not the first serious threat their marriage had sustained. Several years earlier, Hemingway had carried on a flirtation – and possibly more – with Jane Mason, who was beautiful, intelligent, wealthy and, unlike Pauline, an avid angler.[17] Though Mason matched Gellhorn in her beauty, Mason's talent and ambition as a writer remained undeveloped. She was also married and prone to episodes of depression. The unmarried and dauntless Gellhorn, on the other hand, possessed no small amount of natural writing ability and a strong work ethic. Writing to Pauline after the visit, Gellhorn described herself as 'not content' and 'an ambitious girl', and referenced her previous relationship with Bertrand de Jouvenel, a married man, before thanking Pauline for allowing her to become 'a fixture' in the Hemingway home.[18] If Pauline was not yet worried, she should have been.

Hemingway had previously been invited to cover the situation in Spain – which had escalated from rebellion against the democratically elected government to a civil war – for the North American Newspaper Alliance (NANA). It was a good offer: $500 for cabled dispatches, and $1,000 for longer pieces sent by mail, with no limit to the number of stories he could file. These favourable terms made Hemingway the highest-paid correspondent of the war, but it was not simply the money or his interest in Gellhorn that took Hemingway to Spain.[19] Hemingway was already working for the republican *causa*, soliciting donations to supply ambulances and collaborating with Dos Passos, among others, on the anti-fascist documentary *Spain in Flames* (1937).

Hemingway (left) reporting on the Spanish Civil War as a correspondent for the North American Newspaper Alliance (NANA), 1937.

Hemingway and Gellhorn made their separate ways to Spain and met up in Madrid in March 1937. Accounts of their reunion depict Hemingway holding court among fellow journalists and condescendingly announcing to Martha, 'I knew you'd get here daughter, because I fixed it so you could.'[20] In the Hotel Florida, the journalists set up residence, and through the efforts of the New York-born bullfighter Sidney Franklin, who assisted him, or by shooting small game himself, Hemingway managed to procure an enviable stash of comestibles in a city that otherwise faced shortages of just about everything except oranges. He also had two cars and a petrol allowance at his disposal, and got along well with authorities at the Telefónica, a telecommunications building housing the press bureau, where journalists applied for travel permits and submitted their stories to the censors.[21]

In Madrid, which remained in the hands of the Loyalists until the end of the war, the daily shelling was a way of life. In her first article as a special correspondent for *Collier's*, Gellhorn described both the terror of the persistent shelling and how it became a way of life with people who went on 'with the routine of their lives, as if they had been interrupted by a heavy rainstorm but nothing more'.[22] Living in a war zone was, for Hemingway, in many ways a glorious experience. Fellow journalist Josephine Herbst speculated that Hemingway embraced a calling to be '*the* war writer of his age'.[23] Herbst contemplated what about the war in Spain drew Hemingway in and suggested that it

> gave answers that could not be found in that paradise valley of Wyoming where he had fished or even in the waters of Key West when the tarpon struck. What was the deepest reality *there* was in an extreme form *here* [in Madrid], and to get it he had to be in it and he knew it.[24]

Herbst was right that Hemingway was finding new life in Spain: his affair with Gellhorn – which was well known to all in the hotel – fuelled his excitement, and the war was giving him a vast supply of new material to draw upon when he returned stateside.

Hemingway relished his role as resident star correspondent with a beautiful woman at his side and a car at his disposal, and counted among his acquaintances not only writers and film-makers, but International Brigade Commanders Hans Kahle and Pavol Lukács; Chief of the Madrid Secret Police José Quintanilla; and prominent communists like Mikhail Koltsov, who wrote for *Pravda*.[25] Nevertheless, his commitment to the Spanish people was genuine. Hemingway understood, as much as anyone could, what Herbst called 'the diversity of conflicting causations' playing against one another in war-torn Spain.[26] Rebel Nationalist forces – led by General Francisco Franco – were pitted against republican Loyalists, but it was a fractured conflict with shifting alliances and hideous atrocities on both sides: Italy and Germany sent weapons to aid the fascists in what was essentially a weapons test for the coming Second World War; Russian Communists aided the Loyalists, a circumstance that made other nations wary of lending their support; the fascists shelled civilian targets; and the Loyalists murdered Catholic priests who had sided with the Nationalists. Hemingway justified his support of the Loyalists despite the assaults on the clergy and the association with communism, asking why the Church was 'in politics on the side of the oppressors instead of for the people' or even 'in politics at all'. His sympathies lay with 'exploited working people against absentee landlords', even if he did enjoy drinking and shooting with the landlords.[27] He made a similar argument to Pauline's Catholic, wealthy, land-owning family, noting that Spain 'is the dress rehearsal for the inevitable European war' and that he hoped 'to try to write anti-war war correspondence that would help to keep us out of it when it comes'.[28]

Hemingway had already shared this outlook with his *Esquire* readers in his September 1935 letter in which he notes that Americans 'were fools to be sucked in once on a European war and we should never be sucked in again'. The problem in Europe, he rightly argues, is the propaganda and 'patriotic hysteria' supporting Hitler's and Mussolini's regimes.[29] He would change his stance, somewhat, once he got to Spain, however. In a piece written for *Ken* – a highly politicized, Left-leaning magazine that shared its publishers and initial audience with *Esquire* – Hemingway argues implicitly against the policies of the Non-Intervention Agreement (Britain and France, 1936) and Neutrality Act (United States, 1937) and suggests selling munitions to the Spanish – or sending troops – to defeat the Italians and shake Hitler's confidence in his allies. 'It seems we are protected by the oceans so we do not need to care what happens', he writes in *Ken*. Such isolationism, Hemingway notes, cannot last. He speaks directly to the men reading the magazine and threatens them with the 'vomit-stink of transports' on which they will find themselves if Italy is not beaten now, in Spain. Hemingway's warnings went unheeded, and *Ken* lasted only eighteen months.[30]

His NANA dispatches, too, of which 28 are known to have been published in various American and European news outlets, also contained cogent on-the-ground analysis of the war in and around Madrid. The collected dispatches are available under a single cover in the issue of the *Hemingway Review* of March 1988, and editor and compiler William Braasch Watson notes that though Hemingway's reports 'were colored by his unwavering conviction almost to the end that the Loyalists could win the war . . . they were also frequently correct'.[31] Hemingway was, too, working under the constraints of heavy censorship. He may have been recruited by NANA for the value of his famous name, but Hemingway delivered a good product, using his signature brand of experiential reporting to write about military strategy, as well as the human costs of war.[32]

One of those costs was personal. As a sort of 'moral' to his play *The Fifth Column*, written during and about the war, Hemingway suggests, 'people who work for certain organizations have very little time for home life'.[33] The Spanish Civil War had taken him away from Pauline, and in the letter to her parents in which he outlined the necessity of his involvement there, he adds an almost elegiac postscript: 'I'm very grateful to you both for providing Pauline who's made me happier than I've ever been.'[34] Just as when he had been torn between Hadley and Pauline, Hemingway was once again in love with two women at once. Pauline, at home in Key West, kept a household that was conducive to working. She was a willing travel companion, she was a skilful first reader, and she kept the children out of his hair. Worried about his safety in Spain – and likely worried, too, about his attraction to Martha – she initially suggested accompanying Hemingway, but Hemingway insisted she stay behind.[35] The Non-Intervention Agreement made getting from France to Spain, legally anyway, difficult enough that Pauline would have had trouble accompanying him had she pressed the issue, which she did not.

Gellhorn, meanwhile, was with him in the fray: in Madrid; in New York at the Second American Writers' Conference, where he gave a rousing anti-fascist speech to a packed house; and at the White House, where they screened Joris Ivens's film *The Spanish Earth* (1937) for the President and First Lady. The speech, printed later that month in the *New Masses*, declares: 'we are in for many years of undeclared wars', and 'there are many ways that writers can go to them'.[36] Hemingway's passionate involvement in Spain signalled to his previous critics that he was finally going to turn to writing politicized fiction, and indeed his next novel, *To Have and Have Not* (1937), gestured in that direction.

To Have and Have Not, about Harry Morgan, a Key West small boat captain compelled by financial hardship to become a smuggler, was cobbled together from two previously published short stories and a new third instalment.[37] Hemingway's only novel set in the United States, and containing themes that highlight the plight of the working man, it is not his finest work nor even the best example of his political convictions. Bruccoli suggests this work actually poked fun at the social problem novel and that Left-leaning 'fellow-travelers' didn't get the joke.[38] Indeed, the book gives a glimpse at the ineptitude of such a novelist who sees Morgan's wife on the street, misreads her character utterly and decides to include her in his conventional novel about a textile factory strike. Nevertheless, the shortcomings of *To Have and Have Not* more likely indicate what Hemingway had been saying for years, that to write 'truly', he had to ignore the critics and do what pleased him. Only then could he write a book that might also satisfy his readers. The book also demonstrates the difficulty in adapting one genre into another. There is plenty of good writing in the book – Humphrey Bogart would later be perfectly cast as Harry Morgan in Howard Hawks's film adaptation of 1944 – but its seams are visible. Later on Hemingway conceded these faults but stood by it as a generally 'good book', better than the critics said if not as good as he would have liked: it was, he reflected to the journalist Lillian Ross in 1948, 'Jerry built like a position you fortify quickly and with errors but declare to hold'.[39]

The Fifth Column, Hemingway's only full-length play, is another significant but ultimately unsuccessful attempt by Hemingway to write about politics during this period. Composed in the Hotel Florida, where he kept the typescript hidden under a mattress – to protect it from the frequent bombardments and the prying eyes who might not have appreciated that the play 'admits that Fifth Column members were shot' – the play is significant mainly as the sole full-length representative of Hemingway's work in the genre and as an artefact of the war.[40] Hemingway, in his younger days an avid theatre-goer, clearly understands the technical aspects of staging, and he offers the audience a swaggering secret operative whose foil is a hapless war correspondent. Insider knowledge is, as in other Hemingway works, a valuable currency, but 'in Madrid everybody knows everything often before occurrence of same'.[41] The play eschews heroics: the operative Philip Rawlings is successful in his work, and, as a result, the audience watches as a German fifth columnist is tortured. As Hemingway notes in the preface to the play, published in *The Fifth Column and the First Forty-Nine Stories* (1938), he leaves the question of morality open to interpretation – and criticism. The play is a product of its time, he notes, and better work about the war will have to be written afterwards.

By the time the play made it to the stage, the war was over and the Loyalists had lost. Meanwhile, a Hollywood screenwriter had bowdlerized the script, rewriting the female lead as a helpless rape victim who falls in love with her attacker, Rawlings. Hemingway hated the adaptation but proved unable to dissociate his name from the production. The hassles of getting it performed – its first producer died, the next was unable to fund the production – may well explain why Hemingway never wrote another play. By the time it was staged in March 1940, audiences were not interested in lost causes and old news: the play ran for only 87 performances, and critical response was mostly negative. Hemingway grumbled that he should have just written the thing as a novel.[42]

The play had been written from a war zone, but once Hemingway returned stateside, it was time to put his days as a propagandist behind him and get to work on his first major novel in ten years. Though he had published some short stories set in Spain, he had been saving other material for something bigger. He needed now to sort out his home life so that he could find the time, space and spirit to attempt the task. All in all, Hemingway went to Spain four times, and by the time he came home for good in the autumn of 1938, the idea of home was irrevocably changed. Pauline, in an earlier attempt to make Hemingway's domestic scene as pleasant as possible, had put in a swimming pool and built a wall around the property to keep curious tourists at bay; but if she thought these walls could also keep Hemingway in, she was proved wrong.[43] Unable to work at home in Key West, in the spring of 1939 Hemingway began spending most of his time in Cuba. There he began the novel that would become *For Whom the Bell Tolls*, the critical and commercial success that he, Scribner's and the American reading public had longed for since 1929.

8

Notes on the Next War, 1939–44

Hemingway began working on *For Whom the Bell Tolls* in March 1939, writing in a rented room in the Hotel Ambos Mundos in Havana, a location that allowed him some respite from Key West, which had grown from a depressed backwater into a tourist attraction in only a few years. The location also initiated the inevitable separation from Pauline, and allowed him to be with Gellhorn.[1] Though he would maintain his address at the Ambos Mundos to keep up the appearance of propriety, he and Gellhorn soon rented a dilapidated farmhouse set on 15 acres in the village of San Francisco de Paula. The house, known as the Finca Vigía, had been built in 1886 and needed a great deal of repair, but Gellhorn fell in love with the mango grove in the yard and the huge ceiba tree out front on which orchids and bougainvillea grew in abundance.

Gellhorn set about restoring the property into a more livable condition and worked on her own novel about the annexation of Czechoslovakia while Hemingway threw himself into his tale of the Spanish war. He said little of the novel to Perkins except that work on it was steady and unfettered. When he needed a break, he went fishing, but he allowed no distractions, even bowing out of a commitment to a fishing tournament in order to devote his full attention to the book.[2]

As long as the work was good, life was good, and throughout 1939 the typescript grew steadily. Hemingway was nevertheless subject to occasional bouts of guilt or doubt, and confessed obliquely in a letter to Hadley (who was now happily remarried to journalist Paul Mowrer), 'I never do what I shouldn't just to do it . . . Important thing for me to do is not get discouraged and take easy way out like your and my noted ancestors.'[3] This letter is one of many such hints of the spectre of suicide that haunted him his whole adult life. Even when things were otherwise going well, guilt over his betrayal of Pauline was enough to send his mind to dark places, and he recalled, nostalgically but also painfully, the 'fine time' spent with Hadley in the Black Forest when they were first married.

Any pretences about Hemingway's affair with Gellhorn were set aside in the autumn when he and Martha vacationed together in Sun Valley, Idaho. By Christmas even Pauline's parents knew the marriage was over, and he wrote to them in a disingenuous attempt to blame Pauline's sister Jinny for the unravelling of his marriage – she had supposedly worked to turn Pauline against him – and, more honestly, to assure them that he would continue to take care of Pauline and the boys financially.[4] When his relocation to Cuba became permanent, Hemingway had his possessions moved out of the Whitehead Street house, bringing some items to Cuba and storing crates full of manuscripts and other papers at Sloppy Joe's bar, some of which would not be retrieved until after his death.[5] So far, Hemingway had written two major novels and had had two wives, and now he was at work on the third major novel and biding his time until he could marry the third wife. Hemingway was not yet divorced from Pauline before Martha playfully signed a letter to him 'Martha Gellhorn Hemingway' and referred to him as her 'present and future husband'.[6]

The couple had at that point not experienced any major friction, and this brief time between the Spanish war and total war in Europe represented a period of calm in their life together. Yet Martha, however happy she was in Cuba, could never stay in one place very long. In November 1939, she left on a trip to Finland, covering the

Russo-Finnish war for *Collier's*, and though her letters indicate that she missed Hemingway terribly, they also suggest that the couple's relationship was typically happiest when they were apart. In the reality of daily life, their personalities often clashed, and Martha would eventually prove loath to subordinate her own ambitions and interests as Hadley and Pauline had done. The public, however, would from this point on regard her mainly in terms of her association with the more famous author, a circumstance she would come to regret.

In March 1940, a review in *Time* magazine of Gellhorn's novel *A Stricken Field* extolled the author's 'too beautiful' face and 'distracting' long legs, and it noted the similarities between Gellhorn and Dorothy of *The Fifth Column*. The article also announced that Gellhorn was 'headed for San Francisco de Paula, Cuba, where Ernest Hemingway is wintering'.[7] Their names had appeared together in print before, in an item mentioning journalists covering the Spanish Civil War and in reviews of Gellhorn's earlier work, but this was the first mention in print of any personal relationship between Gellhorn and her 'great & good friend, Ernest Hemingway'.[8] Martha, Hemingway and Pauline were all outraged by the article.[9] Hemingway's divorce from Pauline – on grounds of desertion – wouldn't be finalized until November, but it was now on the record that the marriage was over.

As he had done with *A Farewell to Arms*, Hemingway struggled to write the ending of the new novel. Just as he had been compelled to wrap up the loose ends of Frederic Henry's life in rejected versions of that novel's conclusion, so too did he attempt to write an epilogue to follow Robert Jordan's death. Ultimately, however, he abandoned these planned extra chapters and let *For Whom the Bell Tolls* end much as it had begun, with the protagonist lying on the pine needles of the forest floor. The novel was published on 21 October 1940 and was dedicated to Martha Gellhorn. On 21 November 1940, they were married in Cheyenne, Wyoming. The event was reported in

Life magazine and illustrated with photographs by Robert Capa. Two large photographs bookend the piece: in the first, Hemingway beams at Gellhorn, who smiles out at the camera; in the last, he happily displays a pheasant he has shot.[10]

Unlike *The Sun Also Rises*, a *roman-à-clef*, and *A Farewell to Arms*, which takes place against a background so historically accurate it can be plotted upon battlefield maps, *For Whom the Bell Tolls* escapes, somewhat, the de facto autobiographical criticism that has surrounded the other novels. Though some of the characters bear a resemblance to Hemingway's acquaintances – the heavyset, unwavering Pilar recalls the portrait of Gertrude Stein in 1906 by the Spanish artist Pablo Picasso, and any number of International Brigades soldiers could have inspired Robert Jordan – the action itself and even much of the locale is fictitious.[11] Nevertheless it shares the feeling of authenticity that is the hallmark of Hemingway's work. One *Newsweek* reviewer called it '*the* book about the Spanish war', and Hemingway had made a point of learning the tactics of guerilla warfare, but Jordan's mission – to blow a bridge with dynamite – would have been highly irregular and a veritable suicide mission.[12] The importance, instead, is not so much in the mission itself – what is one fewer bridge in the grand scheme of things? – but in the imperative to act and the importance of the individual. While *For Whom the Bells Tolls* is, in some sense, the follow-up to *A Farewell to Arms*, it is also its antipode. Both novels are love stories set against a background of war, but there is an essential political difference: Frederic Henry's desertion and flight to Switzerland in the earlier novel 'endorsed isolationism and antijingoism', while Robert Jordan's last stand 'on the eve of the next world war . . . argued for commitment and war'.[13] It is a call, rather than a farewell, to arms that looks towards the coming world war. Isolationism, Hemingway had argued throughout the 1930s, was impossible, and audiences were finally ready to listen. Hemingway drew the title of the novel as well as its epigraph from John Donne's

'Meditation xvii', which states that 'No man is an *Iland*, intire of it selfe; every man is a peece of the *Continent*, a part of the *maine*'.[14] The message did not go overlooked by the book's earliest critics. A *New York Times* reviewer called it 'the first major novel of the Second World War', and acknowledged that Hemingway's earlier conviction had come to pass: 'the bell that began tolling in Madrid four years ago is audible everywhere today.'[15]

Indeed, the book was loved by critics and readers alike. The novel was a staggering success, finally winning over the massive audience Hemingway had long expected but failed to achieve. It was chosen as a Book of the Month Club (BOMC) main selection, a boon that guaranteed huge sales even as it was, Perkins groused privately to Fitzgerald, a 'stamp of bourgeois approval'.[16] That Hemingway had been willing to tailor the book to fit the needs of the club – leaving out obscene words and taking suggestions from Perkins and Charles Scribner III, grandson of the company's eponymous founder – suggests that he was more than willing to attain that approval, or at least the financial benefit associated with it. Where he had resisted such concessions in the past, this time he allowed nothing to impede bringing the book out to the widest audience possible. Knowing that his marriage to Pauline was ending – and, with it, the financial security afforded by the Pfeiffer family fortune – Hemingway had to make sure that this next book would support the lifestyle to which he had grown accustomed.[17] Selection in the BOMC also ensured a faster turnaround on his first royalty payments along with word-of-mouth advertising from club members. Even without the looming prospect of divorce, Hemingway needed a best-seller to affirm his identity as a great writer, and though he had expressed ambivalence about the BOMC in the past, this time he capitalized on the exposure the club offered. Scribner's, too, worked to ensure the success of the book.[18] A vigorous advertising campaign, coupled with the BOMC exposure, made the novel an immediate best-seller. All told, Scribner's printed 693,486 copies of the novel, and it brought Hemingway earnings of more than $300,000 – more than $100,000 of which came from the sale of the movie rights, a record sum.[19] In both critical and commercial metrics, it was his most successful book yet, selling 'like frozen Daiquiris in hell'.[20]

For Whom the Bell Tolls had seemingly unlimited mass appeal, but it was no hack job. The book is also technically innovative. Its most obvious distinguishing feature is Hemingway's use of the archaic second-person pronouns 'thee' and 'thou', which he used to defamiliarize dialogue ostensibly occurring in Spanish and to denote the distinction – indistinguishable in modern English – between familiar and formal forms of address. Also new to this book is a 'splitting technique' that Hemingway perhaps internalized when editing *The Spanish Earth*. While *The Sun Also Rises* and *A Farewell to Arms* had been linear, following the trajectory of their protagonists with little deviation, *For Whom the Bell Tolls* exhibits a cinematic narrative structure that breaks up the story into scenes, featuring different characters and locations.[21] This new structure is significant: not only does the book depart from the one-sidedness of Hemingway's previous war correspondence, it calls the authenticity of the 'eyewitness account' itself into question, demonstrating to the reader 'the limited nature of witnessing'. These various perspectives serve another thematic purpose as well, allowing the reader to understand the 'dysfunction' of the Loyalist factions as it is played out on a smaller scale by Pablo and company.[22]

The elements that set the novel apart from what Hemingway had done before are also the elements that drew criticism. Those who thought Hemingway's work during the 1930s was the dawn of a 'new Hemingway', a political author who understood 'the necessity for human solidarity', were disappointed.[23] Hemingway's journalism for NANA had been decidedly pro-Loyalist, and the pieces in *Ken* veered towards propaganda, but the novel, written about – rather than for – the cause, drew criticism from some corners for its perceived disloyalty. At one time, Hemingway had been wilfully one-sided in his views, even cutting ties with John Dos Passos when he dared to raise questions about a friend who had gone missing in Republican territory. Now, however, Hemingway was ready to admit that wrongdoing – and virtue – happened on all sides, and he was prepared for the criticism he knew would ensue, even taking out a temporary subscription to the *New Masses* so that he might read the condemnations.[24] Indeed, the magazine published a review by Alvah Bessie, veteran of the Abraham Lincoln Brigade and a former acquaintance of Hemingway's, which expressed the reviewer's disappointment in Hemingway's wasted talent and his betrayal of Spain in general and of André Marty, Commissar of the International Brigades, in particular. Bessie writes:

> Many expected that Hemingway's experience in Spain would so inflame his heart and his talents, that his long-announced novel of that war would be both his finest achievement and 'the' novel about Spain. It is not. It is his finest achievement only in the sense that he has now perfected his extraordinary technical facility and touched some moments of action with a fictional suspense that is literally unbearable. But depth of understanding there is none; breadth of conception is heartbreakingly lacking; there is no searching, no probing, no grappling with the truths of human life that is more than superficial.[25]

Bessie's criticism only hardened over time, and he wrote in 1952 that Hemingway 'shockingly betrayed' the Loyalist cause and that the book 'cruelly misrepresented' the Spanish people and 'maliciously slandered' the International Brigades.[26] Hemingway appears to have been untouched by Bessie's criticism, which he had anticipated. He had known all along that the book presented a complicated truth, 'things that people with party obligations could never write and what most of them could never know or, if they knew, allow themselves to think'.[27]

Hemingway, unamused by the Hawaiian custom of greeting visitors with flower leis, and Martha Gellhorn, en route to China, February 1941.

The biggest snub, however, came not from left-wing critics but from the conservative Nicholas Murray Butler, who, as president of Columbia University, held veto power over the Pulitzer Prize selections. The committee had overwhelmingly picked the novel to receive the prize for fiction in 1941, but Butler had the last say, and he refused to make the award.[28] Other notable fiction in 1940 included the late Thomas Wolfe's *You Can't Go Home Again*, Carson

McCullers's debut *The Heart Is a Lonely Hunter*, Walter Van Tilburg Clark's western *The Ox-Bow Incident* and William Faulkner's *The Hamlet*, but no prize in fiction was awarded that year. Publicly, at least, Hemingway shrugged off the slight, and, in any case, he had made a fortune – at least until it came time to pay his income taxes and to dole out Pauline's alimony.

Hemingway kept careful track of his earnings and his expenses, and was understandably dismayed that his hard-earned financial success was sucked up by the u.s. government at a tax rate of up to 70 per cent for earnings in 1940 and 1941, when the bulk of the profits from *For Whom the Bell Tolls* came through.[29] The problem was not merely that the sudden influx of wealth pushed him into the higher tax bracket – while unfortunate for the earner, such a circumstance was both legal and fair. Rather, as Hemingway and his lawyer Maurice Speiser argued, he was being taxed at a much higher rate than if the earnings were computed as having been the product of several years' work. Hemingway's lawyer used the author's case as an example in a memo to Congress supporting a reform of the tax code. The writer of 'an outstanding American book . . . offered for sale to the public in December 1940', Speiser and his co-author argued, had spent years researching and preparing the book – and incurred numerous expenses along the way – yet had to pay tax on these earnings as the aggregate product of one fiscal year. Furthermore, the author was able to claim only the expenses from the year of publication when taking deductions. The Revenue Act of 1942 passed, making it possible to spread earnings across several years, but it was too late to help Hemingway hold on to his earnings.[30] 'If anyone asks the children what their father did in Mr. Rooseveldts war', he groused to Pauline, 'they can say "He paid for it."'[31]

He grumbled, too, about the $500 monthly alimony payments to Pauline, which were an irksome requirement given her family's great wealth. He was further infuriated to discover that Scribner's drew from his royalties to cover Speiser's fees for an ultimately unsuccessful (and absurd) copyright infringement case brought against him and several major movie studios.[32] Whenever he finished a book, he worried that he might have nothing left in him. However, as he had done his whole life, Hemingway tended to overstate his financial hardships, operating with a sense of caution born out of his middle-class upbringing and exacerbated by the unpredictable nature of his profession. He wrote to Hadley that 'when you get older you have to have a steady something to live on between books – books get further apart as you get older if you write only good books.'[33] His letter to Hadley is wistful and nostalgic. He bemoans the bad luck of making a fortune when the tax rate is so high, but he also notes his good luck of having experienced Paris in the 1920s with her: 'Imagine if we had been born at a time when we could never have had Paris when we were young.'[34] He was just 43 years old and was in good health, but he was already thinking about mortality, not least of all because the previous few years had seen the deaths of numerous friends of his generation.

The recent deaths of F. Scott Fitzgerald (1940), James Joyce and Sherwood Anderson (both 1941), in particular, underscored the vast distance between his younger self of the Paris years and the familiar character he was more and more frequently inhabiting in both public and private spaces. Fitzgerald had died suddenly of a heart attack in his Hollywood apartment, leaving behind an ambitious, unfinished novel (*The Last Tycoon*, 1941), but to hear Hemingway tell it, Scott had given up on life and settled into artistic complacency. Hemingway claimed to Perkins that Fitzgerald's 'heart died in him in France, and soon after he came back, and the rest of him just went on dying progressively after that'.[35] Hemingway's judgement says more about his own fears than it does about Fitzgerald. Edmund Wilson, who helped bring Fitzgerald's posthumous novel into print, wrote in *The Atlantic Monthly* that Hemingway of the 1930s had passed 'into a phase . . . occupied with building up his public personality'. This Hemingway, well known to the public as a handsome sportsman with an 'ominous resemblance to Clark Gable' had become 'his own worst-invented character'.[36] In a revision of his essay, Wilson notes that *For Whom the Bell Tolls* offers a corrective to the cult of personality that Hemingway had allowed to grow up around himself, 'externalizing in plausible characters the elements of his own complex personality', yet even so, Wilson suggests, the story 'lends itself all too readily to the movies'.[37]

Following the success of *For Whom The Bell Tolls*, Hemingway wrote little, and it was with some initial reluctance that he turned to the work that had supported him during artistically lean times in the past: journalism, or, more specifically, war correspondence. It was Gellhorn who pushed the issue, cajoling Hemingway to make a 'honeymoon' of her assignment to cover the Second Sino-Japanese war for *Collier's*. Hemingway followed her lead and contracted with *Time* publisher (and former fishing buddy) Ralph Ingersoll to write articles for *PM*, an upstart New York daily with a liberal slant, and in February 1941 the pair arrived in Hong Kong via a short stopover in Hawaii. Gellhorn would later dub Hemingway 'UC', short for 'Unwilling Companion', in her humorous account of their trip in *Travels with Myself and Another* (1978), and the experience was, for both of them, generally unpleasant. Even the dauntless Hemingway was uncomfortable in the squalid accommodations, but he 'delighted' in the ubiquitous firecrackers and enjoyed meeting the locals and sampling cuisine that Gellhorn couldn't even bear to hear described.[38] Gellhorn recounts how, on one particularly harrowing domestic flight, as the Chinese passengers around them screamed and vomited and Gellhorn was 'racked by guilt' for having led them to this certain death, Hemingway focused on recapturing the gin that had flown out of his cup: 'I didn't lose a drop', he boasted, unfazed as both the plane and his drink seemed to defy the laws of physics.[39]

They were in China more than three months, but Hemingway gained little there in terms of raw material for future writing. The hectic pace of the trip, the complexity of the politics involved, the obtuseness of the officials they met and the general foreignness of the culture may have kept Hemingway from understanding China in any fundamental sense and thus kept him from ever writing about it in any significant work. The main importance of the trip was his recruitment by the U.S. Department of the Treasury to provide intelligence about how the Kuomintang was spending U.S. aid and to report on travel conditions along the Burma Road and Irrawaddy River.[40] The couple had a private audience with Chiang Kai-Shek and Madame Chiang and a clandestine meeting with Communist leader Chou En-lai. Gellhorn later confessed that neither she nor Hemingway knew much of anything about the politics of China, but they followed through after the trip with U.S. Intelligence officers and 'were called Cassandras as usual and branded fellow-travelers as usual'.[41] Hemingway was relieved when the trip was over, as he had earned nearly nothing after taxes and gained little new material for his fiction.

As Gellhorn and Hemingway had seen at first hand, the world was already at war, with fighting in Europe, Asia and North Africa, but Americans still held on to the belief that the United States could remain out of the fray. That belief changed on 7 December 1941, when Japanese aircraft bombed the U.S. Naval base at Pearl Harbor in Hawaii. The United States declared war on Japan the next day, and by the end of the week, the country was at war with Germany and Italy as well. Hemingway, who heard the news as he and Martha were on a road trip through the American Southwest, was outraged that military officials had allowed themselves to be surprised by the attack. He had known all along that war was inevitable, and just as surely he felt the country would be at war for many years to come.[42]

The ecclesiastical verse that had given *The Sun Also Rises* its title held true as a new generation was summoned to an old war. Hemingway had been eighteen years old when he signed on with the ambulance service during the First World War, and now his eldest son Jack, still 'Bumby' to his father, had himself just turned eighteen. This fact may have weighed on Hemingway's mind: in September 1940 the Burke-Wadsworth Act – the military draft – had been signed into law, requiring men aged 21 to 36 to register, and that December Hemingway wrote to Hadley that their son ought to put off college for a year because with the war 'comeing so soon to kids that age' it was important that he experience a 'good life first'.[43] Again Hemingway's advice was prescient, for on 11 November 1942, the 24th anniversary of the First World War armistice, the draft age would be lowered to eighteen. Appropriately, he would dedicate *Men at War* (1942), an anthology of the literature of war, to his sons, and in 1943 Jack began his commission as a lieutenant in the Military Police.[44]

In the preface to *Men at War*, Hemingway writes that he 'hates war and hates all the politicians whose mismanagement, gullibility, cupidity, selfishness and ambition brought on this present war and made it inevitable'. He gets in yet another dig at the 'betrayal of the only countries that fought or were ready to fight to prevent it', namely Spain and Czechoslovakia; however, now that the U.S. was in for the long haul, he proclaims, 'there is only one thing to do. It must be won.'[45] Still on hiatus from any long-term writing endeavours besides his work on the anthology, Hemingway took on a project more fantastic than anything he had written about in his fiction: to blow up a bridge with a backpack's worth of dynamite seems like a perfectly sensible operation compared to Hemingway's real-life wartime sub-chasing activities.

With oil refineries and bauxite mines in the region, the Caribbean was a target for German U-boat attacks, and hundreds of ships were sunk by enemy fire during 1942. Underprepared for the threat, the U.S. government recruited private citizens to loan their sea-craft to the defense of the Atlantic and Gulf waters from Norfolk, Virginia, to Houston, Texas.[46] Though based out of Cuba, Hemingway arranged the approval of U.S. government officials to outfit the *Pilar* with the necessary equipment, and trolled for German submarines. He hoped to get close enough to lure a U-boat to the surface, where he and his team would shoot at it with machine guns and a bazooka and attempt to toss an improvised explosive device onto its conning tower.[47] Trolling for U-boats was not his only espionage work during this time period. In 1942 Hemingway had recruited a number of locals for a counter-intelligence operation to ferret out Spanish fifth columnists exiled in Cuba. Though his activities had the support of local U.S. agents, J. Edgar Hoover, director of the FBI, argued that Hemingway's qualifications as a spy were 'questionable', given the famous author's poor judgement and tendency towards drunkenness.[48]

Martha, who barely tolerated these shenanigans, took off again on another *Collier's* assignment, island-hopping in the Caribbean to investigate how local populations were affected by the war. Before she left, she reminded her editor that though her credentials were written for 'Martha Hemingway,' her articles were 'always to be signed Martha Gellhorn, always'.[49] She returned to Cuba for a time, and the two authors' daily lives criss-crossed as Hemingway set out for weeks at a time on his submarine-chasing missions, leaving Martha at home to work on her latest novel. When they were both at home, they often got into intense arguments. One night, as Gellhorn was driving a drunken Hemingway home from Havana, he slapped her across the face; she responded by carefully driving the car into a ditch and leaving him to find his own way back to the Finca.[50] She also drew his ire when she arranged for some of the cats that occupied the property to be neutered while he was out sub-chasing. Gellhorn hoped to keep the teeming, inbreeding population under control, but Hemingway thought his pets had been unmanned.[51]

Finally, Gellhorn left for Europe to report on the war there, and despite her repeated requests, Hemingway declined to join her. When she was unable to persuade him by any other means, she tried flattery, declaring him a 'very great writer' and suggesting that he might get another important book from the raw material. His refusal would be 'a great general loss for future time, for all people who need and love to read', she implored.[52] As for herself, she explained, she had to be there to see the war first-hand, and if she returned to Cuba – as he had requested at least as often as she had begged him to go to Europe – there would be nothing of herself left with which to love him. In December 1943, their letters were still loving, but both sides were building towards an ultimatum. That ultimatum came to Gellhorn in March via cable, and she recalls that Hemingway demanded to know 'ARE YOU A WAR CORRESPONDENT OR WIFE IN MY BED'.[53] He would not like the answer.

9

The Battler, 1944–7

Hemingway's reluctance to report on the war did not stem from cowardice or laziness. Hemingway delighted in dangerous situations and was miserable when idle. He felt a deep connection to France, was fascinated by war and was in need of a new big writing project, so his initial hesitation to head to the European theatre proved perplexing both to Gellhorn and to the biographers who would later study his life. Carlos Baker suggests that Hemingway was hindered by his conviction that no good writing could happen during a war and that this war could go on for another decade. Feeling that he would be lucky if he had one good novel left inside himself, Hemingway was prepared to wait out the war, lonely and bored.[1] Bernice Kert quotes Patrick Hemingway's reflections that, having beaten the odds in previous wars, Hemingway felt he had earned the privilege not to put himself in harm's way.[2] Michael Reynolds argues that the middle-aged Hemingway was uninterested in, yet again, observing a war from the sidelines. He had spent most of his First World War duty in the hospital, and during the Graeco-Turkish War and the Spanish Civil War, he had been a reporter. As a young man, his poor eyesight had kept him out of the armed services, and at 44, with a bum knee and no formal training, his military prospects were even slimmer. Now he would be hard pressed even to keep up with the younger journalists.[3] Peter Moreira suggests that the author's espionage activities in China, followed by the covert operations in Cuba and on the *Pilar*, had captured his imagination so thoroughly that he had little interest in anything else, including writing.[4] For its part, the Office of Strategic Services (OSS) – with whom his son Jack was now affiliated – felt he was 'too much of an individualist' to work for the military.[5] All of these explanations likely played a part in Hemingway's initial reluctance to go, though a stubborn determination to win the war of attrition at home cannot be overlooked either. Finally, he had to admit that his choices were quite limited: stay in Cuba and wallow in self-pity or obtain the proper credentials and go off to war as a correspondent. Ultimately, Gellhorn and Hemingway both capitulated: she finally came back to Cuba, and, once she was home, he decided to go to the war. Theirs was in no way a joyous reunion or a peaceful compromise.

Hemingway arranged an assignment as a front-line reporter for *Collier's* – a move that effectively demoted Gellhorn. Hemingway did not in any literal sense steal Gellhorn's job – though she certainly saw it that way. The rules for accreditation were restrictive, and women were not allowed on the front lines, so Gellhorn would not have been able to work as the main correspondent for *Collier's* in any case. However, Hemingway's move was duplicitous, even punitive. Of any number of publications that would have been happy to feature a Hemingway byline, he chose Gellhorn's employer, and he used his contacts to reserve a spot on a flight to Europe only for himself, leaving Gellhorn to make a longer and far more dangerous crossing by ship.[6]

When Gellhorn finally arrived in London, the couple's reunion recalled their encounter in 1937 when she caught up with Hemingway in Madrid. There, too, she had found him surrounded by a gang of admiring listeners, and he had annoyed her by publicly taking credit for her successful journey. This time the encounter was even more unpleasant. Finding him hospitalized with a concussion sustained in a car accident, Martha was unsympathetic: both Hemingway and the driver had been drunk when the car hit a water tower during a blackout. When Gellhorn found him 'holding court

Hemingway with an unidentified soldier during the Second World War. As a war correspondent he was forbidden to give orders or take up arms, but he almost certainly violated these terms.

as usual' from his hospital bed, she offered no sympathy and left him to fend for himself, thus making her the first woman since Agnes von Kurowsky to initiate a break-up.[7] She was unaware that he had already begun a flirtation with Mary Welsh Monks, a correspondent for *Time*, who would become the next and final Mrs Hemingway. Even if Gellhorn had known about Mary, she likely would not have cared, and she told Mary years later that it had been a great relief when she discovered the liaison because she knew she was finally free.[8] Gellhorn then set out to cover the war with or without Hemingway's – or *Collier's*, or the War Department's – approval.

The reporters stationed in London – Hemingway and Mary included – had all been anxiously awaiting word of the coming invasion. When it finally began, Gellhorn sneaked aboard a hospital ship and crossed the English Channel. She joined the medical personnel on the beach, helping to bring in the wounded and generally making herself useful. Gellhorn's reward for her gutsy achievement was to have her story held for weeks and her credentials suspended. Her piece on the ship full of wounded soldiers did not appear in *Collier's* until the issue of 5 August 1944; meanwhile, Hemingway's first-person account of the D-Day invasion, which he had observed from a landing ship, was published on 22 June. None of these details mattered to Gellhorn, who hitched a ride to Italy with an RAF pilot and spent the rest of the war as a rogue and roving correspondent. To her dismay, however, she would never really be free from the more famous author's '(odious) light', and for the next five decades she 'suffered professionally wickedly from being always noted as his third wife, as if that was [the] high point, not [her] work'.[9]

Hemingway's D-Day account is at once a fine piece of experiential reporting and an unabashedly self-centred approach to one of the most important events in American history. No one played so great a role in the piece as Hemingway, not even the military personnel he was writing about. According to Hemingway, a gust of wind took their map, but luckily he had already studied it carefully, committing it to memory. He advises 'Andy' (the lieutenant junior grade who, in turn, calls him 'Hemingway') on their location and then on their strategy for avoiding mines. He even suggests disregarding the orders of the commanding officer and continues offering advice throughout the piece – advice which, if the article is to be taken at face value, was consistently proved correct. How the young lieutenant actually felt about the know-it-all celebrity reporter aboard his boat remains a matter of speculation, but the piece is as evocative as it is self-serving, and Hemingway

Mary Welsh Monks in uniform. Hemingway met the fellow war correspondent while they were on assignment in London during the Second World War, and she would become his fourth and last wife.

proclaims 'if you want to know how it was in [a landing craft vehicle] on D-Day when we took Fox Green beach and Easy Red beach on the sixth of June, 1944, then this is as near as I can come to it'.[10] The reader could easily overlook the fact that, unlike Gellhorn, Hemingway had not actually landed on the beach. His role at D-Day, however, was minor compared to his subsequent actions with the u.s. Fourth Infantry Division in Rambouillet, France, about 37 kilometres (23 miles) southwest of occupied Paris – behaviour that he tried to downplay in testimony before the Third Army's Inspector General.

War correspondents were non-combatants, and all were required to wear an insignia on their sleeves, caps and helmets identifying themselves as such. These journalists carried an honorary rank of captain, but were forbidden to take up arms or command troops. These rules gave reporters freedom to circulate between both GIs and officers and were intended to protect reporters should they be captured by the enemy. Rumours that Hemingway had violated these protocols reached Colonel Kent A. Hunter, a public relations officer for General Patton, and Hemingway's conduct was investigated.[11] The investigation sought to determine whether Hemingway 'stripped off correspondent's insignia and acted as a colonel', 'had a room with mines, grenades and war maps' and 'directed resistance patrols', all of which 'violate prudential rights of correspondents'.[12] In November he was summoned to the headquarters of the Inspector General of the Third Army to be interviewed about the role he had played.

In an unpublished, narrative version of his testimony, 'Ernie' (aka 'Papa' and 'Hemingstein') confesses to the reader that he perjured himself under orders from a member of General Patton's staff.[13] When Hemingway was officially questioned, he denied all allegations, and there is no definitive proof on the record that he directly and intentionally violated the conventions that governed the conduct of war correspondents – although it is almost certain that he did. The undisputed account of events is that Hemingway encountered a group of free French resistance fighters at Rambouillet, and took charge of assisting them in their Intelligence activities, relaying their findings to the OSS. He claimed that his fluency in French (a fluency he consistently exaggerated) and his intimate familiarity with the landscape from having bicycled around this part of the country (some twenty years earlier) uniquely qualified him for his unconventional role. He wrote about these exploits, with some dissimulation, in the issue of *Collier's* of 30 September 1944: 'War correspondents are forbidden to command troops, and I had simply conducted these guerrilla fighters to the infantry regiment command post in order that they might give information.'[14]

The article was innocuous enough to pass the censors and his own editors, and it was this version of events that Hemingway supplied to his interrogators, with some lines of his testimony repeating passages from the article nearly verbatim. Hemingway explained away the allegations, testifying that he wore no war correspondent's insignia because the hot weather had driven him to remove his outerwear and that he had not at any time taken up arms. Any honorifics given him by the troops, he claimed, were in an unofficial, affectionate capacity. He admitted storing arms in his room, but pointed out that doing so was not technically against the rules, and he argued that his trips out with the irregulars to gather intelligence fell within the permissible activities of a correspondent looking for source material. The testimony exonerated Hemingway in more ways than one. Rather than exaggerating his heroics – as the D-Day piece had done – the Rambouillet episode shows Hemingway downplaying his role as a participant in events and gives him a certain credibility that he otherwise might have lacked. That the intelligence gathered around Rambouillet was used to plan General Leclerc's advance on Paris also justifies Hemingway's use of the first person plural in 'How We Came To Paris' (*Collier's*, 7 October 1944) – and secured him the right to claim the 'liberation' of the Travellers Club and the Ritz hotel bar, where he enjoyed a well-deserved drink on 25 August 1944.[15]

The tide had turned in the European theatre, and in a love letter to Mary Welsh written from Belgium, where he was attached to Colonel Charles 'Buck' Lanham's 22nd Regiment, Hemingway claims September 1944 as 'the happiest month' of his life.[16] His professional relationship with Lanham had evolved into what would be a lifelong friendship, and his flirtation with Mary had become a full-fledged love affair. In his letters to her, he alludes to a common future. That both of them were still legally married to other people seemed a matter of little concern, despite the fact that all parties involved were journalists travelling in the same circles: Mary

accredited with *Time*, her husband Noel Monks working for the
(London) *Daily Mail* and Gellhorn still filing stories for *Collier's*
despite her lack of paperwork. In a letter to sixteen-year-old Patrick,
Hemingway writes that he has heard little from 'Marty' and 'would
be glad to never see her again'. Meanwhile, he notes that he has
been seeing a 'fine girl' he has nicknamed 'Papa's Pocket Rubens'
and alludes that she is to be part of a 'wonderful life' to come.[17]
Patrick, at boarding school, was given the task of passing along to
the younger Gregory any of this news that he was old enough to
understand – how difficult it was for Patrick himself to read seems
not to have concerned Hemingway, who was riding a manic high
of the Allied victory in France and his new romance with Mary.

   Wartime photos of Mary in her correspondent's uniform show
her to be petite, pert and cheerful. Compared to the tall, lithe, self-
possessed Gellhorn, Mary was, in the vernacular of the early 1940s,
'stacked up'. Like Gellhorn, Mary was also a skilled journalist, but
unlike her predecessor, she was content to let Hemingway 'be the
writer of the family'.[18] In March 1945 Hemingway headed back to
Cuba, where he waited for Mary to join him, and for news of
Bumby, who was being held by the Germans as a POW. Trying to get
his drinking back to pre-war levels – alcohol was his 'best friend and
severest critic' – Hemingway was finally ready to get back to work
on his fiction.[19] For nearly a decade, he had carried around in his
head the rough outline of a story about a Cuban fisherman who
loses the best catch of his life to sharks, and he told Max Perkins of
an ambitious plan to write a book about the war that covered the
land, sea and air.[20]

   The fear that he might one day have nothing left to write had
haunted him since the earliest days of his career. Nearly two decades
before, when he was still in his twenties, Hemingway had written
that 'lots of American writers are through before they're thirty and
most of them are finished by forty five'.[21] Now Hemingway was
himself 45 years old, and he had written no new fiction since *For*

Whom the Bell Tolls. However, the fallow period of the early 1940s was not just the result of ageing or a dried-up creative well, Hemingway's metaphor for writer's block, or simply a product of his fame. The writer's block, the 'black ass' moods – Hemingway's slang for his periods of depression – as well as the violent outbursts that increased in frequency and ferocity in the years following the war, are signs of the serious mental health crisis that would lead to his ultimate self-destruction.[22] Troublesome aspects of his personality, such as his mood swings and occasional angry outbursts, became a more regular occurrence, and his better qualities – his bonhomie and sense of humour – were overshadowed by his growing irritability and, later, paranoia. Hemingway, Mary, Lanham and his other friends, admirers and fans, had no way of knowing it, but the end of the Second World War was the beginning of the end for Hemingway.

Hemingway's difficulty writing during the 1940s and '50s was as much a symptom of his depression as it was the cause: Hemingway was depressed because he struggled to write and he struggled to write because he was depressed.[23] This 'Catch-22', a term coined, appropriately, in the wake of the Second World War by novelist Joseph Heller, tormented the author. The root cause of Hemingway's depression cannot be identified in retrospect with any certainty, though his alcoholism, his fame, his participation in three wars and a family history of mental illness all likely took a toll on him physically and mentally. Another likely source of his writer's block and violent rages could be the numerous concussions Hemingway sustained throughout his life. The concussions may have directly or indirectly contributed to his eventual suicide as well. Research on chronic traumatic encephalopathy (CTE) – neurodegeneration occurring as the result of chronic head injuries – is ongoing, but the most recent findings are consistent with Hemingway's biography. Symptoms of CTE include 'depression' and 'irritability', as well as 'emotional lability, inappropriate behavior, paranoia, outbursts of aggressive behavior and explosivity'.[24] Those suffering from the effects of CTE 'have been described by family and friends as being more irritable, angry, or apathetic, or as having a shorter fuse', and the 'onset of CTE is often in midlife'.[25] All of these symptoms apply to Hemingway in his later years, and the moody and erratic behaviour suggests that the numerous concussions had caught up with him. If Hemingway did suffer from CTE, the condition, which can impair cognition, memory and verbal acuity, makes sense of the difficulty Hemingway had writing in the last years of his career. It also explains his ultimate fate: recent research shows that 'increased suicidality appears to be a particularly salient symptom' of the condition as well.[26] This speculative diagnosis also provides, in retrospect, a sympathetic explanation for his otherwise inexcusably cruel behaviour, the brunt of which was born by Mary.

The exact number of concussions Hemingway sustained throughout his life is unknown, though there were more than a dozen, some of them serious.[27] He had played football in high school and enjoyed boxing (and the occasional non-sporting fist fight) throughout his life. The car accident in London had been particularly damaging, resulting in blinding headaches and requiring stitches, and, just as he seemed to have shaken off the effects of that injury, he hit his head again, this time in a motorcycle accident. Leaping, or perhaps thrown, from a motorcycle after encountering a German anti-tank gun, he hit his head on a rock hard enough to induce double vision and to bring back his headaches.[28] When he returned to Cuba after the war, he was in good spirits and claimed to be in better physical shape than when he had left, but this last war had taken its toll.

Back at the Finca, he was soon joined by Bumby – now almost always called Jack, who had recently been liberated from the POW camp – and Mary, who had begun divorce proceedings from Monks. Hemingway's own divorce from Gellhorn would follow soon after. Hemingway spent his mornings working, and, on the surface, all was well. However, Hemingway still experienced lingering effects from his two most recent concussions, and another car accident resulted in yet another head injury. 'I am getting tired of getting hit on the head', he would later complain.[29] Mary, who made a concerted effort to adapt to life at the Finca and to run a comfortable and efficient household, nevertheless experienced bouts of unhappiness. It didn't help that Hemingway insisted on keeping Martha's picture on display. When they married in March 1946, Mary spent the wedding night alone, both of them seething from an argument earlier in the day.[30]

Nevertheless, Mary was determined to make the marriage work, and she hoped to give Hemingway the daughter he had always wanted. Hadley and Ernest had been married only long enough to have one child together, and Pauline's Caesarean deliveries required that she not bear any more children after Patrick and Gregory. Gellhorn may have had an abortion during her involvement with Hemingway, or a previous abortion may have left her infertile.[31] In any case, Gellhorn was not going to give him any children. Just shy of her 38th birthday when they married, Mary was in a hurry to get pregnant. Together she and Hemingway made plans for the daughter they hoped to call Bridget.[32] Mary became pregnant soon after they were married, but the pregnancy was ectopic, and when the growing embryo ruptured her fallopian tube, she nearly died from internal bleeding. The surgeon treating her was ready to give her up for dead, but Hemingway, reacting with grace under pressure, gave orders to cut into her veins and personally worked the plasma bag until she came back to life.[33] Once Mary was on the road to recovery, Hemingway joked to Lanham that he was not trying to come off as 'Dr Hemingstein the Great Emergency Handler' but rather was 'fascinated by how much can be done to f— fate rather than accept it'.[34] Even as Catherine Barkley had been doomed by fate in his fiction, in his own life Hemingway was determined to outmanoeuvre death. Mary soon made a complete recovery, but she would later learn that her remaining fallopian tube was blocked, making her infertile. Whether Hemingway would have been a better father to his wished-for daughter than he had been to his sons cannot be known, but Mary, an only child who never had any children of her own, judged herself harshly as 'a failed member of the human race'.[35] Meanwhile, Thomas Hudson, a semi-autobiographical character Hemingway was developing around this time, reflects: 'it is much less lonely sleeping when you can hear children breathing when you wake in the night.'[36]

Writing was work he still purportedly enjoyed – or at least that's what he told Malcolm Cowley, who had edited *The Portable Hemingway* and was at work on a long biographical sketch for *Life* magazine. 'Do you suffer when you write?' he asked Cowley. 'I don't at all. Suffer like a bastard when don't write . . . But never feel as good as while writing.'[37] Hemingway produced page after page of work – he reported to Perkins in March 1947 that he had over 900 manuscript pages.[38] His writings during this period would split into several disparate parts, including what would become *Across the River and Into the Trees* (1950) and *The Old Man and the Sea* (1952), and the fragments that would be edited posthumously into *Islands in the Stream* (1970) and *The Garden of Eden* (1986). Though scholars have tried to sort out the order in which these later works were conceived and executed, no definitive timeline exists – nor could it, as work on the books was not linear. Hemingway's body of work from the end of the Second World War until his death is, rather, a self-consciously Proustian 'serial sequence' concerned with the 'portrait of the artist'.[39] The portrait that emerges from these various manuscripts is, however, complicated and incomplete, though there may be a thematic unity – a theme Hemingway himself spelled out as 'the happiness of the Garden that a man must lose'.[40] Hemingway eventually came to think of his body of work 'as a single, fluid text', and as his career evolved, he recognized the difference between writer, one who writes, and author, one who publishes. Hemingway abandoned the single-minded focus of an author – the focus that had brought *The Sun Also Rises*, *A Farewell to Arms* and *For Whom the Bell Tolls* into print – to take on the more complicated work of a writer.[41] Hemingway was not merely boasting when he claimed to have 'moved through arithmetic, through plane geometry and algebra' and to be 'in calculus'. He was trying to explain what he was doing, and if his readers, his publisher, his wife or the critics could not understand, 'to hell with them'.[42] Hemingway was working, and working well, and that was enough. During this time he may, too, have begun to think about writing his memoirs – something he had always alluded to as a project to be saved for when he had exhausted all other topics.[43] Hemingway could now have the last word: Stein had died in 1946, and Pound, who had been arrested on charges of treason for the pro-fascist radio broadcasts he had made in Italy, had been declared unfit for trial and was incarcerated in a federal psychiatric hospital. It would still be another decade, however, before the manuscript that would become *A Moveable Feast* received Hemingway's sustained attention.

Toiling away on this ambitious and unrealizable magnum opus, Hemingway was incensed when he read a news item that William Faulkner had publicly claimed that Hemingway 'has no courage'. Hemingway rightly took offence at the jibe, but for all the wrong reasons. Faulkner, in an informal talk to students at the University of Mississippi, had claimed that Hemingway had 'never crawled out on a limb', suggesting that, though he ranked his rival among the top five modern American writers, Hemingway was risk-averse.[44] Faulkner was likely referring to Hemingway's linear narratives and economy of style. The pronouncement made its way into the *New York Herald Tribune*, and Hemingway, taking the comments literally to mean that he lacked personal courage, tasked Lanham with sending Faulkner a rebuttal that related his bravery during the last war. Had Faulkner been privy to what Hemingway was trying to do with his current land-sea-air project, he might have reconsidered his claim. Or perhaps he would have let it stand – the two authors clashed aesthetically, and, regarding Faulkner's 'mellifluous' literary experiments, Hemingway groused that he just wished Faulkner would write something readable.[45] Hemingway and Faulkner exchanged letters directly following Faulkner's receipt of Lanham's encomium, and Hemingway was mollified by Faulkner's apology, but Faulkner remained perplexed that his comments had been so misinterpreted.

As he continued to toil away on the book (or books), Hemingway was losing control of his own mythos. Publishing nothing new but remaining in the public eye nonetheless, Hemingway relied on the sale of film rights and on reprints and translations for his income.[46] Such sales were a sign of his enduring success, but that success came with a price, and he now had to confront criticism that he was washed up. A *Time* magazine questionnaire from 1947 asked him if 'the "Hemingway influence" [had] declined', and his succinct, ungrammatical reply demonstrates both self-awareness and self-deprecation: 'Hemingway influence only a certain clarification of the language which is now in the public domain.'[47] Unsurprisingly, then, his next published novel would deal with the painful experience of a man who has outlived his relevance.

10

The Tradesman's Return, 1947–51

Hemingway's personal relationships over the past two decades had been tumultuous, but his professional relationship with his publishing house had remained relatively stable. Though he had often complained that Scribner's could be doing more to promote his work, he never exhibited any serious intention of moving to another firm. When Maxwell Perkins died suddenly in June 1947, Hemingway wrote to reassure Charles Scribner III that he would remain loyal.[1] Maybe Hemingway was inured to any sense of loss, having already outlasted so many of his early contemporaries, for in his letter to Scribner, Hemingway seems surprisingly unmoved by the death of his long-time editor. Offering brief condolences, Hemingway goes on to discuss business and to share some tips for making a good martini.

The publisher welcomed the news of Hemingway's loyalty despite not having had a book by its star author since *For Whom the Bell Tolls* in 1940. Hemingway remained an important asset to Scribner's catalogue, and Scribner wrote to Hemingway himself to ask that he and Wallace Meyer take over Max's role as primary contact and editor, respectively. He reassured Hemingway that they would continue to honour Perkins's hands-off approach and that the firm would be working hard to push its 'seasoned books', specifically a proposed illustrated edition of *A Farewell to Arms*.[2] The relationship was symbiotic: with no new book to offer, Hemingway needed Scribner's to market his back catalogue, and as Hemingway's celebrity continued to grow even during this fallow period, Scribner knew that the next book, whenever it should arrive, would be a guaranteed best-seller.

Back in Cuba, Hemingway was hard at work, writing each day and keeping track of his word counts. He was satisfied when he produced around 500 words a day, sometimes more. He was also at work to improve his physical well-being, taking blood pressure medication, trying to get his weight down from 114 kilograms (252 lbs) and limiting his alcohol consumption, which had been heavy during the war.[3] Just as he found some satisfaction in reporting to Scribner how many words he was producing, so too did he gain some validation in watching his weight drop, and he kept a running tally on the bathroom wall. Meanwhile, Mary was settled in, learning Spanish and taking charge of the household so that Hemingway could focus on his work. Unannounced visitors to the Finca were a common enough occurrence that Hemingway complained of being compelled to hang up a sign informing interlopers, in Spanish, that 'Mr H receives no one without a previous appointment.'[4] However, one unannounced visitor in particular went on to make himself indispensable to the writer. In the spring of 1948, A. E. 'Ed' Hotchner arrived in Havana on an assignment for *Cosmopolitan* magazine to recruit Hemingway to write an article called 'The Future of Literature'. Hotchner, sheepish and awestruck, got through to the famous author, who plied him with frozen daiquiris and took an immediate liking to him. Hotchner was young, only 27 years old, and had worked as a documentary film-maker for the Army Air Corps during the war.[5] Like Hemingway, Hotchner was disappointed when poor eyesight kept him out of combat service, and like Hemingway's first three wives, he had St Louis roots. He was smart without pretension and a skilful editor without genius, and he fell easily into the role of pupil, companion and agent. Though nothing ultimately came of the proposed *Cosmopolitan* article, Hotchner would land a bigger fish for the magazine, negotiating serial rights to the first new Hemingway novel in ten years.

That novel grew out of the work Hemingway produced while in Italy from September 1948 to May 1949. The inspiration for the long-anticipated novel was largely Hemingway's unrequited infatuation with a beautiful young woman 30 years his junior, and it was a story of ageing, disability and death. It was also about the costs of practising one's trade – in the case of the protagonist, Colonel Richard Cantwell, the trade was soldiering, but Cantwell's struggle applies to the work of the professional writer as well.

The Italy trip was, in essence, an extended vacation, even as Hemingway skipped most of Mary's sightseeing excursions and kept to his writing schedule. Not there to make a living or to cover a war, Hemingway was, more so than during any point in his life to date, an American tourist. As nostalgic as he may have been for his days in the ambulance service or for the picturesque poverty of his Paris apprenticeship, 49-year-old Papa Hemingway enjoyed a degree of luxury he would have neither had access to nor even wanted in his earlier years. He brought his Buick across the ocean with him to Italy, where the Hemingways hired a chauffeur, and they stayed in the Gritti Palace, the most expensive hotel in Venice.[6] If Hemingway's accommodations were of a different calibre than those his earlier self might have chosen, his companions, too, were different. Hemingway had long disported himself with the nouveaux riches like the Murphys and celebrities like the actor Gary Cooper, but in Italy he found himself associating with members of the aristocracy.

On a rainy weekend hunting trip with Count Carlo Kechler and Barone Nanyuki Franchetti, Hemingway first encountered Adriana Ivancich, the eighteen-year-old only daughter of an old family hard hit by the war. Her long, dark hair wet and tangled, Adriana was in need of a comb, and Hemingway broke his own in half and offered it to her.[7] It was more than a friendly gesture – this story of their fireside encounter is just one of many that evidence Hemingway's 'erotic fascination with hair'.[8] He was immediately captivated by the young woman whose brother, Gianfranco, had worked for the American Office of Strategic Services and whose father funnelled supplies to Allied supporters and had been killed – murdered, the family believed – by a corrupt fellow partisan.[9] Aristocratic, tragic and darkly beautiful, Adriana became Hemingway's next muse, even though their meetings were limited to the occasional lunch date, and they were always in the company of mutual friends.

In December the Hemingways relocated to Cortina d'Ampezzo, a ski resort, and there Hemingway had yet another mishap: he was stricken with an eye infection and required hospitalization. Doctors feared it might spread to his brain, and Hemingway feared blindness.[10] He made a complete recovery, but rumours circulated that this most recent brush with death convinced him to abandon, for the present, the longer project so that he might get another novel into print as soon as possible – 'the Hemingway credo in a nutshell'.[11]

Returning to Venice, Hemingway violated his old mandate that to write about a place he had to leave it behind, and set about writing a novel set in Italy. Comfortably situated back at the Gritti, Hemingway poked fun at Sinclair Lewis, also a guest there, for drinking heavily, writing prolifically and 'peer[ing] at whatever was 3 starred in Baedaker', but the two writers had more in common than Hemingway would have liked to admit.[12] Hemingway, too, was writing 'vastly', and so he punished Lewis as he had punished Anderson and Fitzgerald, by skewering him in print. Hemingway's barely anonymized portrait describes a man whose face is as 'pock-marked and blemished as the mountains of the moon seen through a cheap telescope . . . like Goebbels' face, if Herr Goebbels had ever been in a plane that burned, and had not been able to bail out before the fire reached him'.[13] It was, even for Hemingway, a low blow, and in his letters to Scribner, Hemingway was still making use of the old boxing trope to talk about which writers he could 'beat'.

He felt he had bested Lewis, but there were always challengers. Scribner, in turn, worried about libel issues and was in the awkward position of being the mutual publisher of both Hemingway and Gellhorn, who came off little better than Lewis in early drafts of *Across the River and Into the Trees*. Hemingway warned Scribner: if Gellhorn dared to sue, or tried to take him on in print herself, he would 'fix her up for posterity, or whatever they call the place, like a trussed pig on a wheel-barrow in China'.[14] The reference to China, site of the couple's unpleasant 'honeymoon', reveals that the source of his bitterness was personal, not literary. In the published novel, Cantwell dismisses his ex-wife as having 'more ambition than Napoleon and about the talent of the average High School Valedictorian'.[15] The reference to Gellhorn was clear, at least to Scribner, to whom Hemingway had groused that Martha was 'a social worker with great ambition'.[16]

Hemingway had reason to be annoyed with Gellhorn: a Hemingway-esque figure shows up as an oafish war correspondent in Gellhorn's farcical play *Love Goes to Press* (co-written with Virginia Cowles, performed in 1946). He may also have been resentful that other writers were getting their Second World War books out ahead of his: 1948 saw the publication of Gellhorn's *The Wine of Astonishment*, as well as *The Young Lions* by Irwin Shaw, a fellow war correspondent and one of Mary's former love interests.[17]

Whatever his motivation, when Hemingway returned to Cuba in May 1949, he worked steadily on the new novel, first in the new tower that Mary had designed and commissioned, and, when he missed the hustle-and-bustle of daily life in the main house, standing at his bookshelf as various home improvement projects took place around him.[18] He rushed the novel to get it ready in time to meet the *Cosmopolitan* deadlines, but both Mary and Scribner had misgivings about the story, which followed the demoted American colonel and veteran of two world wars as he spends the last day of his life duck hunting and reflecting on his love for a teenaged Italian noblewoman.

Hemingway pauses to pet a pair of hunting dogs in Venice, 1948. Hemingway's love for his cats is well known, but he was fond of dogs as well and even remarked to Mary that while cats were the couple's 'longest suit', dogs were 'trumps' (Mary Hemingway, *How It Was*, p. 244).

The similarities his heroine, Renata, bore to Adriana were unmistakable, and no one could overlook the fact that both Hemingway and his protagonist were 50 years old. And, like Hemingway, the Colonel had lost count of the number of concussions he had suffered. Aside from certain physical and geographical details, however, the love story was a complete fiction. Under no circumstances did Hemingway and Adriana ever consummate their relationship in a gondola, a hotel room or anywhere else for that matter. Understanding that Hemingway was infatuated with an unattainable fantasy, Mary endured Adriana's presence in their lives. She was less forgiving of his carousing with Havana prostitutes during this same time period, even as she reluctantly made the acquaintance of Hemingway's 'long-time occasional girlfriend', Leopoldina.[19]

There were other flirtations as well, but despite her husband's transgressions, Mary was determined that she would never be ousted as Mrs Hemingway, not by Adriana nor by any other woman. Her tenacity made up for her never being immortalized in a published story or novel, as the other women in his life had been, and she would ultimately be his literary executor – of that she was reasonably certain. In the meantime, Hemingway dedicated the book 'To Mary With Love', fulfilling a promise from the earliest days of their courtship. Outwardly, Mary was pleased, but the gesture fell short: it was, she thought, 'his poorest book'.[20]

Conscious of Hemingway's sensitivity to criticism, however, Mary cheered him on. In a letter to Scribner, Hemingway claimed that after reading 121 pages of the work in progress, Mary 'hasn't been any good for anything since. Waits on me hand and foot and doesn't give a damn if I have whores or countesses or what as long as I have the luck to write like that.'[21] Mary tells a different story in her memoir. She worried that the first part of the book was 'just ducks and marshes', and, upon reading a manuscript draft of the second half, she knew it was not as good as Hemingway had been confidently reporting to her. She recalls that she was 'unhappy' with some of the 'banal' dialogue and Hemingway's 'mysterious lapse of judgment' regarding the May-to-December romance, but she said nothing to Hemingway in the hopes that the editors would help him resolve the book's weaknesses – they did not.[22]

Hemingway may have known, too, that *Across the River and Into the Trees* was flawed, and though he told Scribner that he wanted 'to play this horse to win', he anticipated a harsh response from critics: 'If the critics don't like it . . . it is more or less their ass because we run the bulldozer over them with the next book.'[23] Unfortunately, he had already borrowed against the next book, repurposing part of the larger manuscript he had previously been working on to bulk up the current project with an account of the battle of Huertgen Forest.[24] This strategy had not worked for him in the past, when he built *To Have and Have Not* from spare parts, but up against tight deadlines – Scribner's and *Cosmopolitan* were already promoting the forthcoming serialization – his typical daily output of 500 words would have delayed publication well into the new year or beyond.

The serial ran in *Cosmopolitan* from February to June 1950; meanwhile, Hemingway continued tinkering with the novel, which Scribner's released on 7 September. However, even these changes could not hide what the editor, Wallace Meyer, felt were fundamental flaws. The editors did not try to force Hemingway to make revisions other than those necessary to avoid libel suits, but Meyer confided to Scribner that 'the book hasn't the idea of a novel. There isn't the essential core there.'[25] The novel deals with the usual theme of death, but, unlike anything Hemingway had written before, it also looks at ageing. His protagonist has survived two wars and been divorced, and now his heart is giving out. Knowing that his fatal heart attack is imminent, Cantwell chooses to spend his last day on earth reflecting on the choices he has made in life and the choices that have been made for him.

With a few notable exceptions, the critical reception was not positive. The English novelist Evelyn Waugh responded to the 'smug, condescending, derisive' attacks on the work, not by praising the book itself, which he conceded might well be Hemingway's worst, but by reminding readers of Hemingway's contributions to literature. The qualities critics had praised in *The Sun Also Rises* were just as present in *Across the River and Into the Trees*, he argues. Waugh, who did not know Hemingway personally, suggests that something about Hemingway as a personality rubbed critics the wrong way. The combination of Hemingway's boorish and anti-intellectual public persona – visible especially in Lillian Ross's infamously unflattering *New Yorker* profile of him from 13 May 1950 – and the old-fashioned chivalric sensibility of his characters proves incompatible with the 'supercilious caddishness which is all the rage' in post-war literary circles.[26]

The American novelist John O'Hara, who, at age 45, was a near-contemporary of Hemingway and Cantwell, was one of the few reviewers to praise the book. He did so with embarrassingly effusive hyperbole, naming Hemingway the 'most important author living today, the outstanding author since the death of Shakespeare'.[27] E. B. White, then best known as an essayist for the *New Yorker*, parodied the novel in that publication with the light-hearted 'Across the Street and into the Grill' (14 October 1950). With its lunch-counter setting, the parody recalls Hemingway's own long-ago send-up of Anderson and Stein in *The Torrents of Spring*.

Those who disliked the book were put off by what they saw as a rehashing of old themes and not enough distance between author and subject – Cantwell was, they felt, too obviously auto-biographical. Hemingway complained to Scribner that the dust jacket had made him look like 'a cat-eating Zombie', and he shrugged off the negative reviews with unusual equanimity.[28] He was equally unfazed by any acclaim the book had received, and he told Scribner he would have been happier with O'Hara's praise had the man actually understood the book.[29] What most critics – including O'Hara – failed to see is how *Across the River and Into the Trees* is a retrospective on the author's career. His editor, Wallace Meyer, was correct in his private assessment that Hemingway was in 'a transition phase, physically speaking' and 'a transition phase as a creative artist'.[30] Hemingway's years of hard living and many hard knocks were catching up to him, but he was attempting to write a book far more complex than any he had yet attempted. Meanwhile, Meyer's – and everyone else's – unwillingness to read the new novel as anything other than a tired retelling of the same old Hemingway story exposes the very problem the story illustrates: both Hemingway and Cantwell live to see themselves discounted by authorities in the institutions to which they had devoted their careers.

Cantwell's backstory, which biographer Jeffrey Meyers suggests was inspired by circumstances of Hemingway's old friend Chink Dorman-Smith's unjust demotion, reflects, too, Hemingway's own bouncing around in the esteem of the literary elite. Hemingway confronts the uncomfortable realization that, Shakespeare excepted, literary fame is ephemeral, and he creates in *Across the River and Into the Trees* a metafictional elegy to his own career. In addition to more than 25 instances of the word 'trade' – typically in reference to the skilful practices of soldiering and writing – the novel contains tongue-in-cheek references to Hemingway's characteristically short sentences and his disinclination towards adverbs.[31] Hemingway also peppered the book with numerous allusions to his body of work. Some of the references would have been obscure to his contemporaries, alluding to works by titles he had rejected when they were still in manuscript form, but others are buried in plain sight: for example, the book contains three separate instances of the phrase 'in our time'.[32]

Some references are more oblique, but their presence is not mere coincidence, and many of Hemingway's greatest hits are represented. The wind in the duck blind is described as 'rising with the sun' and the Gran Maestro's smile is 'as solid as the sun rises'.[33] A 'blown bridge' makes an appearance in passing, and Cantwell, who, like Frederic Henry, was 'a lieutenant then, and in a foreign army', has 'moved through the different arms of the service as he had moved into and out of the arms of different women'.[34] Like the speaker in *Green Hills of Africa*, Cantwell 'thought in terms that were as far beyond him as calculus is distant from a man who has only the knowledge of arithmetic', and he recalls, if not the snows of Kilimanjaro specifically, then 'les neiges d'antan' ('the snows of yesteryear').[35] In a restaurant that may well be a clean, well-lighted place, Cantwell is served at the table by a boy 'who believed in nothing; but was trying hard to be a good second waiter'.[36] Renata refers to herself as 'the unknown country', an allusion to 'The Undiscovered Country', one of the working titles of *For Whom the Bell Tolls*.[37] In conversation about his ex-wife, Cantwell quips 'that was in another country and besides the wench is dead', an allusion to Christopher Marlowe's *The Jew of Malta* and a phrase that Hemingway had used as both a title to a published short story ('In Another Country', 1927) and included in a list of possible titles for *A Farewell to Arms*.[38] 'Farewell . . . is a nice word', he speculates later.[39] As Jake Barnes had done, Cantwell 'looked at himself in the mirror' while naked, and he watches light reflected from the canal onto his ceiling, 'changing, as the current of a trout stream changes, but remaining, still changing as the sun moved', recalling Nick Adams in 'Big Two-Hearted River', who watched as a trout 'caught the sun, and then, as he went back into the stream under the surface, his shadow seemed to float down the stream with the current'.[40] Other references to Hemingway's ouevre can be found throughout the novel, and, collectively, they create a bibliography of the author's body of work.

At the end of the novel, when Cantwell succumbs to his fatal heart attack, his driver, an impudent soldier who finds Cantwell tiresome, scoffs at the Colonel's dying wish to return the portrait of Renata to the girl. Instead he decides to let the property wend its way 'through channels', guaranteeing that it will be mired in the bureaucracy of the u.s. Army.[41] The novel concludes with the suggestion that ultimately the legacy of a work of art is at the mercy of others, and for Hemingway, that power is wielded by the critics and scholars who were, he felt, as eager to see him fail as they were to read a best-seller. Though he claimed to 'give what all for hereafter', he nevertheless continued his idiosyncratic practice of imagining himself in literary sparring contests with Turgenev, Shakespeare and other dead greats.[42]

For all his posturing in public and in private about taking on other writers, Hemingway's persona had grown larger than his (still considerable) talent could bear, and he knew it. *Across the River and Into the Trees* exposed, as critic Isaac Rosenfeld noted, the 'sad wreck of [Hemingway's] life behind the myth'.[43] Hemingway had certainly contributed to the myth-making, but by the 1950s he had, to no small degree, lost all control over his own public image. In the 1920s Hemingway had been an accessible representative of the 'lost generation' for Americans learning how to become modern; now, in the wake of the Second World War, he was both 'a role model and tonic for the American male who was having trouble adjusting to a postwar suburbanization'.[44] From his poetic experiments in the little magazines of the 1920s to his *Esquire* 'letters' and war correspondence of the 1930s and '40s, Hemingway had largely been in control of his public image. Now, in the 1950s, he was more often written *about* than writing – at least as far as the public knew – and the articles appeared not only in mainstream slicks but in pulp magazines as well. He helped to define American masculinity, and, in turn, the American mythos was working to define him. The unchecked popularity of this public image may have interfered with Hemingway's ability to write, and it certainly impacted the reception of his work by readers and critics.[45]

The critical reception of *Across the River and Into the Trees* had little effect on the author's confidence, however, especially since he made money off the book. Yet Hemingway bristled when his literary rival, William Faulkner, accepted the Nobel Prize in Literature in December 1950. To add insult to injury, Faulkner stopped just short of calling Hemingway out by name in his Nobel address.[46] That his rival had earned the accolade before he himself surely needled Hemingway, but outwardly, at least, Hemingway claimed to be 'pleased' for Faulkner. Perhaps the Academy's slight even spurred him on: 'Bite on the nail Hemingstein, you un-prized non-academied son of a bitch', he taunted himself in a letter to literary critic Harvey Breit in 1952, 'and let's see if you can really write and how far you can take it'.[47] His words were not idle posturing, for he already had a more or less complete draft of *The Old Man and the Sea* contained in the big manuscript. Hemingway was, however, in no real rush to publish, as he could live off money earned from Hotchner's adaptations of his short stories for television.[48] He continued working, updating Scribner's periodically on his progress: by July 1951 he estimated the book to be nearly 2,000 manuscript-pages long, and he suggested to his publisher that, if he were to die, it was in a polished-enough condition that it could be brought out, posthumously, as four separate books.[49] Previously, he had declared that his manuscripts should be burned and that 'posterity can take care of herself or fuck herself'.[50] Now, however, he was thinking seriously about the state of his personal archive and his legacy.

11

The Undefeated, 1951–4

'Men are dying this year who have never died before', Hemingway quipped, but there was less glee in outliving people than his younger self had perhaps anticipated.[1] When his mother died in June 1951, Hemingway did not attend the funeral and wrote to Sunny that he did not wish to have any of their mother's paintings.[2] Then in October Pauline died suddenly of complications from an adrenal tumour – the catalyst for her crash may have been the heated telephone conversation she had with Hemingway earlier that evening regarding Gregory and a recent arrest. Gregory reports in his memoir that the charges against him were drug-related, but he was actually picked up for cross-dressing in public, and whatever Hemingway said to Pauline over the phone left her distraught.[3] Then in February 1952, Charles Scribner died suddenly of a heart attack. The blows dealt by these deaths were only exacerbated by the disconcerting experience of Hemingway finding himself being metaphorically embalmed while still alive: the living author was now, with alarming frequency, becoming the subject of critical study. His antipathy for literary critics was well established, going back to Paris in the 1920s, but the latest books and articles were not by contemporary reviewers or public intellectuals of the sort who had gleefully panned *Across the River and Into the Trees*. Rather, he was beginning to attract greater attention from professors within the academy, and 1952 saw the publication of *Hemingway: The Writer as Artist* by Carlos Baker of Princeton and *Ernest Hemingway* by

Philip Young, a junior faculty member at New York University. Hemingway had initially resisted giving Young permission to quote from his work, but he finally acquiesced, stating that he did not want to be responsible for keeping a man from earning a living.[4] That book, and its 1966 revision, used a psychological approach to read Hemingway's First World War wounding as the primary source of his work and thus set the course for several decades of Hemingway scholarship.[5] Also in 1952, Charles A. Fenton, a doctoral student at Yale, was at work on his dissertation, which considered the role Hemingway's journalism played in his apprenticeship, and he pestered Hemingway with frequent questions.[6] A recent profile by Malcolm Cowley in *Life* and Lillian Ross's profile in the *New Yorker* had been bad enough, but now Hemingway was enduring the horrifying experience of seeing his life written up by people he had never even met.

Hemingway was uncomfortable with being canonized for a variety of reasons, not least of which was the fact that he felt he was an author with several good books left in him – indeed, he had several good books set down on paper, and he continued to wrestle with the unwieldy, experimental and still largely unpublishable manuscripts. He had no ambition, he boasted to Scribner, 'except to be champion of the world' and 'to take Mr Melville and Mr Doestoevsky'.[7]

Hemingway would indeed go on to win a title bout, but the book that would ultimately earn him the Pulitzer and Nobel prizes was not the ambitious and never-finished trilogy but a slim little novella, a story he had been carrying around in his mind since the 1930s. In his *Esquire* letter of April 1936, he related to readers the outline of a tale told to him by Carlos Gutiérrez about an old man fishing alone, who 'hooked a great marlin, that, on the heavy sashcord handline, pulled the skiff far out to sea'. The man had been pulled by the fish for two days and nights. Once he had harpooned the fish and lashed it to the boat, the sharks hit, 'and the old man had fought them out alone in the Gulf Stream in a skiff, clubbing them, stabbing at them, lunging at them with an oar until he was exhausted'. In this rough sketch of the tale, the old man is rescued by fishermen, 'crying . . . half crazy from his loss'.[8] When Hemingway reimagined the story as *The Old Man and the Sea*, he retained the basic elements of the battle between the man and fish, and the man and sharks, but he changed the ending. Hemingway's Santiago does not despair or lose his mind; rather, he returns to his hut, where he goes to sleep and dreams of lions on the beach in Africa. The 'totemic' image of the lions hearkens back to Santiago's boyhood years spent aboard ship, and the dream of Africa offers comfort and restoration.[9] With his thoughts in Africa too, as he worked on *The Garden of Eden* and later his second African book, Hemingway would continue to write, but *The Old Man and the Sea* would be the last book he published in his lifetime.

The Old Man and the Sea felt like the realization of his life's work, the culmination of the poetic exercises that had been the first published work of his Paris apprenticeship. It was 'the prose that I have been working for all my life', he had written to Scribner, a prose style 'that should read easily and simply and seem short and yet have all the dimensions of the visible world and the world of a man's spirit'.[10] Reflecting on his long career, Hemingway remarked to Wallace Meyer, who was his remaining personal connection at the publishing house, that the composition of *The Sun Also Rises* had taken him about six weeks but required extensive revision, while *The Old Man and the Sea*, written in a similarly brief time frame of just eight weeks, had emerged fully formed.[11] The novel that had made his reputation and the novella that would cement it for all time were, in some ways, the two over which he struggled least. The little book need not, he realized, resemble a Russian epic to be good, and he decided to bring it out on its own. After some negotiation about publication dates, the schedule was set: *The Old Man and the Sea* would appear in full in *Life* magazine on 1 September 1952;

Scribner's would publish it one week later, and it was also picked up by the BOMC. The deals with *Life* and BOMC ensured that the book would receive unprecedented exposure, but still Hemingway worried whether availability in these outlets would ultimately hurt sales in stores. His worries turned out to be unfounded. The issue of *Life* officially hit the newsstands on 28 August 1952 and immediately sold out, in some locations the night before. The interest generated by word-of-mouth publicity compelled bookstores to not-so-secretly sell copies ahead of the official 8 September release date as well, and BOMC subscribers eagerly awaited distribution the following day. The audience for this novel was the largest in Hemingway's career: more than 5 million copies of *Life* and 153,000 copies of the BOMC edition were in print, in addition to the 133,650 copies printed by Scribner's.[12] The following year, he sold the movie rights, and two-time Academy Award winner Spencer Tracy signed on to play the lead. In addition to being a popular success, the book was a tremendous critical success as well. Even William Faulkner praised it in print, speculating that 'time may show it to be the best single piece' written by any contemporary author, including himself.[13] Then, in May 1953, the announcement came that Hemingway had won the Pulitzer Prize for fiction for 1952. Hemingway feigned indifference for the accolade, but he could finally enjoy the private satisfaction of being vindicated for the earlier snub.[14]

The professional success and his iconic public persona belied a darker reality of Hemingway's private life, however. Behind the walls of the Finca Vigía, Hemingway had been, increasingly, not the affable if salty patriarch the public knew but rather an abusive husband who berated his wife in front of chagrined family and friends, threw wine in her face and shot his gun at household objects. Mary felt she was witnessing 'the disintegration of a personality' – as, indeed, she was.[15] There are any number of reasons Mary may have stayed in the marriage: perhaps she felt trapped by her own and her ageing parents' financial dependence

Hemingway on guard at his Cuban home, the Finca Vigía, in 1952.

on Hemingway's guaranteed income; perhaps she felt she owed her life to the man who had brought her back from certain death on the Casper, Wyoming, operating table; perhaps she had the foresight to anticipate, correctly, that she would one day be the beneficiary of his 'life insurance' – that is, the rights to his unpublished manuscripts; perhaps she loved him enough to forgive any transgression; perhaps she felt the need to protect him from himself. Or perhaps Mary, like many victims of domestic violence, was convinced that she was to blame for the violent outbursts or was too frightened to leave.[16]

In between the flare-ups of Hemingway's temper, the domestic scene was often a happy one. Mary had worked hard to learn to

Hemingway poses for *Look* magazine photographer Earl Theisen with Mount Kilimanjaro visible in the background, 1953.

enjoy fishing and shooting and even had her own launch called *The Tin Kid*. Unlike Martha before her, Mary had given up her own career, and she devoted herself to making sure nothing interfered with Hemingway's work. Hemingway's private correspondence boasts, too, of Mary's enthusiasm in bed and of their active sex life.[17]

In the wake of his greatest success, Hemingway enjoyed some degree of contentment, and with his finances and his reputation secure, Hemingway allowed himself the luxury of returning to Africa as he had always vowed he would. Mary accompanied him as they revisited sites of Hemingway's youthful adventures along the way, and though Mary was visiting some of these places for the first time, she, like so many others, already knew them intimately as a reader of Hemingway's books.

First they went to Spain, taking in the *feria* at Pamplona, and there Hemingway met Antonio Ordóñez, the son of the bullfighter on whom he had modelled Pedro Romero of *The Sun Also Rises*. They visited the Hotel Florida in Madrid, the nostalgia tempered by the fact that Franco still remained in power. If Mary felt Hadley's, Pauline's or Martha's presence in these places, she declines to mention it in her memoir. After a brief stopover at the Ritz in Paris, the Hemingways headed to East Africa, and Philip Percival came out of retirement to join them on safari in a game preserve where they had exclusive hunting rights. They also made a brief trip to Tanganyika, where Hemingway's son Patrick, a professional hunter, owned a farm. Though Hemingway contrasted himself with the kind of rich white tourists who go on safari 'killing the necessary beasts that represented, in big-game hunting, so many academic degrees', his presence in Kenya was welcomed by the local government for the publicity it would bring the tourist industry, which was suffering as a result of conflict there between Kikuyu groups and white colonials.[18] The trip was also funded, in part, by *Look* magazine, and Hemingway gamely posed for photos. Hemingway's private experience of the safari differed significantly from the version he would publish in *Look*, and his book-length account, first published posthumously as *True at First Light* (1999) and, later, as the less heavily redacted *Under Kilimanjaro* (2005), falls somewhere in between the *Look* piece and the more complicated, unknowable reality that exists apart from Hemingway's reminiscences or Mary's journal and memoir.

Certainly, however, this safari was quite different than the one he had taken with Pauline in the 1930s. When Hemingway wrote about the second safari later, he characterized himself as content, good-humoured and reflective. (It is important to note, however, that this account, while based on true events, is very much the product of the author's imagination, and he surely took many artistic liberties with his recollections.) The book-length account of his trip, which would go unpublished until many years after his death, emphasizes that he was not in Africa, this time, to score the maximum number of allowable trophies. He made some kills and posed for pictures, but in his recollections of the trip, it is Mary who relentlessly stalks a lion and a kind of antelope called a gerenuk while Hemingway looks on. He depicts himself as more interested in meddling in local affairs, working as a self-styled game warden and carousing with the gang of buddies he calls 'the bads' than in stalking game. Hemingway reflects that twenty years earlier he 'had called [the guides] boys' without realizing that he had 'no right' to do so; on this later safari, he saw them as 'friends and brothers' – a group of cronies and advisors whom he likes and trusts. This time, he affords them more respect, noting that 'everyone had his duties and everyone had a name'.[19]

Though his regard for his African guides had become more progressive than in years past, Hemingway showed few qualms about entering into a sexual relationship with a local teenaged Wakamba girl named Debba. Little evidence of the exact nature of the relationship exists beyond Hemingway's own (possibly exaggerated) accounts, so it is impossible to know if his sexual advances were welcome. He certainly leveraged his position as a wealthy foreigner and rewarded the girl with gifts of clothing, and both he and Mary recount one 'celebration' so vigorous that it resulted in a broken bed frame.[20] Hemingway referred to Debba as his fiancée, and imagined fathering a child with her, and Mary, as always, endured the affair patiently if not altogether happily.[21] She took comfort in her own prejudices, certain that Hemingway would not leave her for an African girl whom she derided as dirty, illiterate and interested primarily in the gifts bestowed on her by the wealthy American. Mary did not respond with jealousy but rather worked to keep the marriage bed interesting.[22] Hemingway's desire to marry the girl was motivated by more than 'eroticization of racial otherness'; Hemingway attempted to follow Wakamba customs in his interactions with the girl's family, and this effort suggests the seriousness with which Hemingway undertook the project of becoming an 'honorary Kamba'.[23]

Hemingway's lifelong quest for insider knowledge (and, perhaps, a longstanding desire to be married to more than one woman at once) were born out as Hemingway shaved his head and dyed his clothing in imitation of local customs.[24] Hemingway was playing out a fantasy that in some essential way reconnected him with the Michigan landscapes of his youth. In Africa, he would later recall, they lived in one of the 'mystical countries that are a part of one's childhood', the kind of place that adults can only dream about – and then only if they are very lucky. Yet even in Africa, he could not escape the nightmares that had plagued him since the First World War, 'the real ones that could drench you in sweat'.[25] Like any dream, the African idyll came to an end, though it was hardly the farewell that Hemingway could have anticipated, and it ushered in a period of decline from which he would not recover.

In December 1953, with their safari coming to an end, the couple enjoyed adapting their Christmas celebrations to their surroundings. Mary carefully selected a suitable tree from among the native species and did some Christmas shopping in Nairobi. In a festive and generous mood, they gave presents to all members of their party. Hemingway's gift to Mary was an 'air safari', an aerial tour in a Cessna 180 that would take them over the Serengeti Plain to the Belgian Congo (now the Democratic Republic of Congo). After breaking camp and returning to Nairobi, they embarked on their aerial tour on 21 January. As the pilot, Roy Marsh, flew low above

Hemingway had the unusual experience of reading news accounts of his own death after surviving a plane crash in Uganda. Front cover of the *New York Daily News*, 25 January 1954.

Murchison Falls so that Mary could take photos, the plane hit a telegraph wire and Marsh was forced to make a crash landing.[26] That they survived the ordeal is a testament to the pilot's skill, but the party still faced the difficulty of being stranded in the wilderness of equatorial Africa with a broken radio antenna and few supplies. The next day, they spotted a charter boat and arranged a ride to Butiaba, a small town on the shore of Lake Albert in Uganda. There they boarded a biplane piloted by Reggie Cartwright, who, anxious to get his famous passengers to Entebbe, insisted on taking off that same evening despite the failing light. The plane crashed before it even made it off the makeshift runway, and it caught fire with the passengers trapped inside. Marsh, also a passenger on this flight, helped Mary escape through a window, but the opening was too small for Hemingway. Facing the prospect of a fiery death, he had no choice but to bash the damaged door open with his head, giving himself yet another serious concussion, this time fracturing his skull and damaging his spine in the process.

The seriousness of Hemingway's injuries became apparent to Mary the next morning when she saw that cerebrospinal fluid from his untreated head wound had soaked into his pillow.[27] The archival record of the exact nature of Hemingway's injuries is inconsistent and speculative, but all agree that the injuries were extensive and went untreated for too long. In the days after the crashes, he received only basic first aid, and he self-medicated with alcohol, though he already knew from experience that drinking was contraindicated. There was other collateral damage: in addition to money, passports and other valuables, they lost their camera equipment and the film that had documented their safari.[28] Hemingway had not lost any of his writing, however, because there had been no writing to lose, a lucky circumstance that nonetheless suggests the trip had not been wholly good for him, plane crashes notwithstanding. As far as the public knew, however, Hemingway walked away from the wreckage with his typical bravado, 'carrying a bunch of bananas and a bottle of gin'.[29]

The Hemingways took up residence in a hotel in Nairobi and, despite his considerable pain, Hemingway enjoyed the singular pleasure of reading news stories about the accident. When Marsh's plane had failed to make a planned stop to refuel, a search plane spotted the wreckage but found no sign of survivors. News outlets around the world picked up the story and reported the famous author missing or dead.[30] When Hemingway turned up alive, he made headlines again. These reports, riddled with half-truths and inaccuracies, indicate the extent to which Hemingway's public image had, by this time, separated itself from the real man. The news outlets downplayed the author's actual injuries even as they exaggerated the risks he had faced from elephants and other big game on the ground. The *New York Times* even reported that the

Hemingways had 'crashed into a towering waterfall'.[31] As far as the public knew, Hemingway had proven himself to be indestructible. Hemingway, too, may have believed he would make a full recovery from these injuries just as he had, in the past, bounced back from the mortar explosion or the Wyoming car crash. In his account of the events published several months later in *Look* magazine, he stated, optimistically, that he hoped 'to have fun and to write as well as possible'.[32] In reality, however, the plane crashes had done irreparable harm.

Hemingway had once speculated that, with the sole exception of escaping unendurable physical torment, suicide was like cheating at a one-player card game, and he now wrote in Mary's journal that he was enduring 'Semi-unbearable suffering'.[33] The spectre of suicide had long haunted Hemingway's darker thoughts, and the headlines that had reported his death and his miraculous survival reassured him that his life's work would be celebrated worldwide upon his death. The physical pain of his injuries, coupled with the knowledge of his secure place in literary history, had the potential to set him on a dangerous course. What stopped him was the knowledge that he still had work to do: his unfinished long manuscript, as well as books about Africa and about Paris. As long as Hemingway could still write, life would go on.

12

The Last Good Country, 1954–61

As the African trip drew to a close 'an evil miasma, a foul-smelling deafening raucous bird of destruction and disaster' descended upon the Hemingway party.[1] Hemingway reacted violently to even the slightest provocation, leaving Mary in tears. He remained in his berth for most of the return sea voyage, and, back in Venice, finally received much-needed X-rays. Though he put on an act of health and vigour for reporters, Hemingway remained in a great deal of pain. He was well aware that his 'thinking which sometimes tends toward violence' was the result of his concussion: 'people aren't indestructible even if the journalists say so', he mused to his friend, the art historian Bernard Berenson.[2] Hemingway was not destroyed, but neither was he fully whole, and his outbursts contained brief glimpses of the paranoia that would haunt his last years, such as when he publicly accused his wife of stealing his pocketknife.[3] When he returned, finally, to his Cuban home, he seemed to have aged a great deal more than just one year.

His recovery was slow, but he had returned to his old routine of writing and fishing and was making steady progress on a book about the most recent safari. Soon, however, Hemingway's routine was disrupted once again, but this disruption was quite welcome: early in the morning on 28 October 1954, Hemingway got word that he had won the Nobel Prize in Literature. It was not entirely unexpected news, and Hemingway strongly suspected that his most recent brush with death had inspired the committee to give him the accolade while it still had the chance. Hemingway sent his apologies that poor health prevented him from travelling to Sweden to attend the ceremony in person, but he wrote some remarks to be read on his behalf. With gratitude and humility, Hemingway expressed philosophies of writing consistent with those he had espoused in *Death in the Afternoon* and *Green Hills of Africa*: that the meaning in a writer's work may not be 'immediately discernible' and that a writer must 'try for something that has never been done' – something 'beyond attainment'. Alluding, perhaps, to the protagonist of the book that had secured him the award, Hemingway concluded that a great writer who seeks to achieve something new must go 'far out

The Swedish ambassador to Cuba presents Hemingway with the Nobel Prize in Literature, 1954.

past where he can go, out to where no one can help him'. New here though is the confession that as the author 'grows in public stature . . . often his work deteriorates'.[4] In writing *The Old Man and the Sea*, Hemingway had confronted the critics, but he had also confronted himself and returned to the pared-down sensibility that brought him his early success. Despite its seeming simplicity, the book was also Hemingway's most spiritual, and, fittingly, he gave his gold Nobel medal to the shrine of the Virgin of Cobre, Our Lady of Charity, the patroness of Cuba. This move was more than a charitable gesture, for the book was very much a Cuban story. The bones of the ruined fish are a kind of relic or 'spiritual gift' from Santiago to the villagers who had dismissed him as *salao*, or 'the worst form of unlucky'.[5] So, too, was Hemingway's book a gift to readers worldwide, even though many had lost faith in the ageing writer whose luck seemed to have long run out.

At the end of *The Old Man and the Sea*, Santiago will live to see another day, but Manolo surely knows as he sits by the sleeping man's bedside that there would not be another great fish. Hemingway would have been less sure of his own future prospects, but nearly two years after the African misadventure, Hemingway could still feel the effects of the ordeal, both physically and artistically. As he struggled to regain his physical fitness, work on the Africa book continued mostly unhindered, except by the numerous guests – invited and uninvited – who had invaded his space ever since he became a Nobel Laureate.

Hemingway ended up spending the latter weeks of 1955 and first weeks of 1956 laid up in bed with kidney and liver ailments, and he had no choice but to strictly limit his alcohol intake. He was further distracted from writing by the attempts of a Hollywood crew to film *The Old Man and the Sea* on location in Cuba, and, when the local fish would not cooperate, in Peru. The Peru jaunt was Hemingway's only trip to South America, and it made little impression upon him. Attempts to get suitable marlin footage were unsuccessful, and the

Hemingway was regularly featured as a masculine icon in mens' magazines of the 1950s, as seen in this February 1956 issue of *True: The Man's Magazine*.

director finally opted to use rubber decoys. Hemingway was ultimately as disappointed with the adaptation as he was with any of the previous efforts to bring his novels to the big screen.[6]

In January 1957, Hemingway made a trip to France that was generally uneventful except for the rediscovery of some trunks belonging to him in a storage room of the Ritz Hotel.[7] The cargo of these trunks, left there in 1930 when he and Pauline had moved to Key West, is almost as legendary as that of the lost suitcase of 1922, and Mary Hemingway would later credit the discovery as the inspiration for the sketches that would make up *A Moveable Feast*. Even if he was already working on the sketches before the trunks were found, they offered him a time capsule back to an idyllic past. That younger Hemingway – handsome, vigorous and ready to take the American literary scene by storm – might have recoiled from the image of the old man sifting through the contents of the trunks. That man, who looked even older than his 57 years, was on a range of prescription medications to treat anxiety, sleeplessness and liver problems, and he took supplements including vitamins and testosterone.[8] The young Hemingway had always had a spring in his step; he was a 'boulevard shadow-boxer' in perpetual avoidance of a quick jab from an imagined opponent.[9] This old man was bent, the skin on his face was patchy, and an elaborate comb-over covered his balding head while fooling no one. Meanwhile, the world around him was changing: Hemingway displayed outward nonchalance at the news that the Russians had launched Sputnik 1, the first satellite to orbit the earth, but the Cold War was escalating, and the Cuban Missile Crisis was only five years in the future.[10]

Cuba – with wild orchids and heavily laden fruit trees, hurricanes and the Gulf Stream, Spanish Catholicism and Yoruban traditions, baseball and blood sports – had been Hemingway's refuge and his atelier for many years. The restored farmhouse outside San Francisco de Paula had been an ideal location for working and for not working. It was here that Hemingway shared his home with countless cats and a few beloved dogs, had lived with two wives and hosted numerous friends and flirtations. In the tropical climate, with its unpredictable storms and high humidity, the home was in constant need of repairs, and the famous occupant and his imagined fortune attracted the occasional foreign pilgrim or local burglar.[11] By the late 1950s, Hemingway was growing increasingly annoyed with encroaching real estate developments that catered to tourists.[12] These inconveniences were merely a nuisance, however, compared to the very real threat of revolution to overthrow the Batista government. One night in May 1957, a patrol of soldiers came to the house, looking for imagined enemies. The following morning, the Hemingways found one of the dogs lying dead, its skull bashed in.[13] Hemingway joked to a friend that kidnapping was 'the latest local sport', but by 1958 the situation was serious enough that he confided to his son Patrick that he '[m]ight pull out'.[14] He knew that, even as his celebrity afforded him some protection and many Cubans claimed him as one of their own, he was still wealthy and an outsider and in some danger. When Fulgencio Batista was ousted on 1 January 1959, Hemingway was not sorry to see him go, but he was ambivalent about the new socialist regime, headed by Fidel Castro.[15] He began to consider where he might relocate should it become necessary to leave Cuba.

In Ketchum, Idaho, he and Mary could escape hurricane season, and the hunting was good. The skiing was good too, but Hemingway no longer skied. He was too infirm for that pastime, but, as he reflected in his Paris memoir, skiing had fundamentally changed anyway. With the invention of the chair lift – first put into operation in Sun Valley, actually – people didn't have to walk up the mountain to earn the ride down, as they had in the old days. Hemingway tried to connect skiing and heartbreak in the Paris sketches, but the metaphor wouldn't work. The Paris book was almost ready to publish, but Hemingway struggled to complete this chapter and tinkered with others. 'There is never any end to Paris', he wrote, but everything had changed.[16] A year earlier, with some

Hemingway in his Ketchum home in Idaho in the winter of 1958–9.

help from Hemingway and others, Ezra Pound had finally been
released from St Elizabeth's Hospital in Washington, DC, and
remanded to his daughter's care back in Italy. The anomie of the
so-called 'lost generation', with its Great War and subsequent
Great Depression, had given way to a bigger war, and, in its wake,
the space race, computers, television, fallout shelters, ready credit,
inflation, McCarthyism, Billy Graham, modular homes, beat
poetry, rock 'n' roll, *Brown v. Board of Education* and a conservative
retrenchment that masked the coming political and social upheaval.[17]
Hemingway's 'bunkerlike' Ketchum home, made of cement blocks
but resembling a hunting lodge in its design, embodied its purpose:
it may have looked like a vacation retreat, but Hemingway rarely
hunted anymore, and the house was, essentially, a shelter.[18]

Unfortunately, Hemingway could not hide from the turmoil of
his inner life, and at the beginning of 1959, he was headlong on the
downward slope that inevitably followed a period of significant
literary productivity.[19] Yet to the outside world, there was no
productivity – Hemingway seemed to be 'a near parody of himself

Ernest Hemingway with bullfighters Antonio Ordóñez and Pepe Luis Vázquez in Zaragoza, Spain, summer 1959.

. . . bent on playing the part of a Hemingway character'.[20] Neither the smug critics he loathed nor the growing number of academics embarking on formal study of his work (whom he also loathed) could have guessed at the significance of the projects Hemingway had undertaken, remarkable not just in their vastness but in their complexity and intertextuality. When George Plimpton asked Hemingway, in an interview published in the *Paris Review* in 1958, whether 'a writer's power diminishes as he grows older', Hemingway replied that 'people who know what they are doing should last as long as their heads last'.[21] Unfortunately, the personal demons, the myriad health problems and the distraction of a dangerous summer prevented Hemingway from bringing any of his last manuscripts to completion. His final publication was, instead, an unwieldy journalistic piece on bullfighting.

From May to August, Hemingway followed the bullfights across Spain. He planned to supplement *Death in the Afternoon* with new material, but the project evolved into a long-form piece for *Life*, covering the rivalry between Antonio Ordóñez and Ordóñez's brother-in-law Luis Miguel Dominguín. The story had a built-in narrative conflict as the two men faced each other in *mano a mano* competition, yet Hemingway was covering not just one showdown but rather an entire season of *tauromachia* and was cursed with an overabundance of raw material.

When not on the road, the Hemingways were hosted at the home of Bill and Annie Davis, a wealthy American couple, at their country estate, La Cónsula, near Malaga, Spain. At their various destinations, they were joined by an entourage that now included Valerie Danby-Smith, a nineteen-year-old Irish journalist, and in Pamplona, Hemingway was mobbed by autograph-seeking college students hoping to live out their own version of *The Sun Also Rises*. At La Cónsula, Mary threw Hemingway an extravagant 60th birthday party that included live music, carnival games and fireworks and lasted until morning.[22] Despite the rollicking atmosphere of the birthday party and other festivities, and Hotchner's claim that it was 'one of the best seasons of [Hemingway's] life', Mary was beginning to suspect that the constant travelling and associated *ferias* were taking a toll on Hemingway's physical and mental well-being.[23] Under the guise of getting the Finca ready for visitors and the new household in Ketchum established, Mary departed Spain ahead of Hemingway. Back in Cuba, she enumerated in a long letter the 'neglect, rudeness, thoughtlessness, abusive language' and other cruelties she had suffered and noted her plans to set up a separate residence for herself in New York – a city Hemingway claimed to hate.[24] When Hemingway returned to Castro's new Cuba, he publicly kissed the Cuban flag before an audience of reporters.[25] His reunion with Mary was not so effusive or affectionate, but she nevertheless decided to stay with him.

One source of tension was Hemingway's complete inability to edit down the more than 100,000 words of his bullfighting account

to something publishable. He had taken suggestions before –
as when Fitzgerald suggested cutting Brett's backstory from
The Sun Also Rises – but not since Pound chopped all but two
lines off 'Neo-Thomist Poem' for the *Exile* of 1927 had anyone
edited Hemingway's work for him, and perhaps not even then.[26]
Hemingway had scoffed at the degree to which Perkins had had
to cut Thomas Wolfe's *Of Time and the River*, but now Hemingway
was forced to enlist Hotchner to do something similar to his
manuscript – which now constituted not a supplement but an entire
new book – down to a still-sprawling 54,000 words.[27] *Life* finally
published 'The Dangerous Summer' in two instalments beginning
with the issue of 5 September 1960. Meanwhile, Valerie Danby-
Smith was on the payroll as Hemingway's secretary, and her
principal role – besides being a youthful companion – was handling
the author's correspondence. Hemingway was outwardly hopeful
that, with 'The Dangerous Summer' complete, he could emerge into
a belle époque as he had done before after periods of depression.
He knew, however, that he was as likely to go in the other
direction, continuing his downward spiral towards 'a complete
physical and nervous crack-up'. Aptly, he compared his 'brain
fogged' state to that of the recently concussed Ordóñez.[28]

Hemingway's condition continued to worsen, and he became
increasingly paranoid about perceived threats to his safety and his
finances.[29] Finally, in late November 1960, he sought psychiatric
treatment, and was admitted to the Mayo Clinic in Rochester,
Minnesota. He was checked in as George Saviers, the name of his
Ketchum physician and close friend who accompanied him and
Mary to Rochester, and thus was able to avoid publicity for a few
weeks. When his presence at the hospital was eventually discovered,
the public story was that he was being treated for 'hypertension'.[30]
During his nearly two-month stay, he underwent electroconvulsive
therapy, a treatment for severe depression that induced seizures in
the patient; amnesia was a typical, even desirable, side effect. This

memory loss proved devastating to Hemingway, however, as it stripped from him his fundamental identity. He had once told Hotchner that 'The worst death for anyone is to lose the center of his being . . . to retire from what you do – and what you do makes you what you are – is to back up into the grave.'[31] Seen in this light, the handwritten sign on his hospital room door with which the occupant identified himself as a 'FORMER WRITER' becomes an ominous portent.[32] He was discharged but not cured, and his inability to formulate a few lines for a presentation volume to the newly inaugurated President Kennedy reduced him to tears.[33] The loss of this fundamental part of his identity was devastating, yet it was but one among many causes that led to Hemingway's ultimately fatal depression.

The Bay of Pigs invasion on 17 April 1961, too, may have been a catalyst that pushed Hemingway over the brink. Newswire reports in April 1961 allowed for no middle ground: the Castro regime had aligned with the Soviets and was therefore a dangerous enemy, while the Cuban people, Castro's unwilling victims, were in danger. Despite the Kennedy administration's rhetoric, the Bay of Pigs invasion was not another Normandy Landing in a 'struggle of liberty against tyranny', though the Eisenhower and Kennedy administrations proceeded as if it were.[34] With the authorization of President Kennedy, a U.S.-trained guerilla army made up of anti-Castro expatriate Cubans planned to invade Cuba, garner support from within and set up a provisional government that would be friendlier to U.S. interests, but the execution of the invasion was a debacle. The troops came ashore in swampland, a planned air strike was scuttled and the invaders did not receive the warm welcome they had anticipated.[35] The Hemingways heard the news on the radio and TV, and what they heard could not have been at all encouraging.[36] They surely knew that this breakdown in diplomacy would not soon be sorted out – indeed, the U.S. and Cuba would not attempt to normalize relations until decades later, in 2014. Hemingway, who

Entryway of Hemingway's Ketchum, Idaho, home where he committed suicide on 2 July 1961. Mary Hemingway bequeathed the home to The Nature Conservancy upon her death in 1986.

had briefed one of Castro's aides on how to talk to the u.s. press and who had worked for many years as a war correspondent himself, would have known, too, that he was not hearing the whole story.[37] Still, there was truth to wire reports that Cuban civilians were being taken prisoner, and Hemingway was facing the fact that he might never know the fate of his friends and employees. When u.s. newspapers reported a 'communications blackout' – no phones, no cables, no flights – Hemingway suddenly found himself, in a very real sense, in exile.[38] The same issue of *Time* that had broken the story of his stint at the Mayo clinic also proclaimed 'Castro's Triumph', predicting, accurately, that 'it would be a long time before Cubans, either inside or outside the island, could mount a serious threat to his dictatorship'.[39] Cuba was not simply where Hemingway's house was located; it was his home. His friends, his house, his boat, his books, his artworks, his animal trophies and, perhaps worst of all, the manuscripts he had been working on for the past two decades might be lost to him forever. He had recovered from the loss of his 'juvenilia' in 1922, but these manuscripts were the culmination of his life's work.[40] Not coincidentally, it was around this time that Hemingway became suicidal.[41]

On 21 April 1961, Mary discovered Hemingway in the front vestibule of their Ketchum house, holding a shotgun. Frightened for her own safety as well as his, she talked to him for an hour as she waited for his friend and physician Saviers to arrive for his daily visit. A second incident with the shotgun occurred three days later, and again Hemingway was prevented from harming himself. On his journey back to Rochester, he continued to demonstrate suicidal tendencies. More electroshock treatments followed, and Hemingway – charismatic to the end – convinced his doctor that he was well enough to be released. Mary knew better, but she also knew she could not convince Hemingway willingly to obtain the help he needed, which she believed to be long-term care in a residential facility. Unable to fight that battle alone, she instead took him back home to Ketchum. Mary writes in her memoir that she had locked Hemingway's guns up in a basement storage room, but she stopped short of hiding the keys because she could not bring herself 'to deny a man access to his possessions'.[42] On the evening of 1 July 1961, she recalls, the couple sang a little duet as they made their preparations for bed. The next morning, while Mary slept, Hemingway blew off his cranium with a double-barrelled shotgun.

L'Envoi

For he does his work alone and if he is a good enough writer he must face eternity, or the lack of it, each day.[1]

In *To Have and Have Not*, Hemingway had reflected, presciently it turns out, on

those well-constructed implements that end insomnia, terminate remorse, cure cancer, avoid bankruptcy, and blast an exit from intolerable positions by the pressure of a finger . . . their only drawback the mess they leave for relatives to clean up.[2]

Suicide is a recurring topic elsewhere in Hemingway's work as well: the husband in 'Indian Camp' cuts his own throat; the old man in 'A Clean Well-Lighted Place' had attempted to hang himself but his niece cut him down; Robert Jordan reflects on his late father, a 'coward' and a suicide; Peduzzi in 'Out of Season' went on to kill himself, or so Hemingway claims in commentary in *A Moveable Feast*. This list is hardly exhaustive, and the references to suicide in the author's correspondence are too numerous to mention. His manner of death, then, was in some ways inevitable and expected. News outlets reported Mary Hemingway's claim that his death was accidental, incurred as Hemingway was cleaning his gun, but they did so with between-the-lines scepticism that stopped short of making any potentially libellous claims. The *New York Times*, for example, noted that Hemingway was an 'expert on firearms' and that his father had committed suicide, and quoted the coroner as saying, 'I couldn't say it was accidental and I couldn't say it was suicide.'[3] The temporary dissemblance allowed for Hemingway to have a Catholic burial, which took place in Ketchum Cemetery in a small private ceremony.[4]

Though many people had already ascertained the truth, Mary wanted to keep up the appearance that the death had been accidental. She even went to court to halt the publication of Hotchner's memoir of 1966, *Papa Hemingway*, which revealed the true manner of Hemingway's death. When the court decided in Hotchner's favour, she finally went public, conceding in an interview with an Italian journalist, reprinted in *Look* magazine, that Hemingway's death had been a suicide.[5] The story was subsequently picked up by other outlets, and papers around the world reported as news what many already knew or suspected.

Mary also made headlines only a few weeks after Hemingway's death when the Kennedy and Castro governments, in an astonishing act of cooperation in that political climate, made concessions to allow her to travel to and from Cuba in order to transport Hemingway's private papers back to the U.S. The Cuban government took possession of the Finca Vigía, its contents and the *Pilar*, turning them into the Museo Hemingway, but Mary was able to ship several boxes of manuscripts, correspondence and other personal effects back stateside. The *New York Times* reported that she was on site in Cuba making decisions on what from among the '"hundreds of thousands of typewritten pages" . . . should be kept or destroyed'.[6] Her task was a formidable one, as Hemingway was something of a pack rat, and she can hardly be blamed for wishing to dispose of decades-old bullfighting papers. She may indeed have thrown out interesting papers and ephemera as well, but in the end, Mary brought home the most important items: an extensive collection of archival materials, including the long-unfinished drafts of the big manuscript.

These works would gradually be edited, some more extensively than others, and published in pieces over the next half-century. Hemingway had known that his work would be published posthumously; indeed, he had counted on it, and Mary set about the task as quickly and as conscientiously as she was able. Many of her decisions have been criticized by scholars more familiar with the theories and practices of textual editing than Mary, who was guided by her somewhat limited experience as a journalist and her biased perspective as a widow. Scribner's, too, had a hand in the decisions, and the firm was more interested in editing the works to appeal to a wide audience than in preserving their textual integrity.

The criticism and second-guessing of Mary's abilities began from the moment the task was announced. In a letter to the *New York Times*, the novelist Glenway Wescott, who had the dubious honour of having been immortalized as Robert Prentiss in *The Sun Also Rises*, accurately and sensitively expressed the wishes of serious scholars and readers of Hemingway:

> Indeed as [Hemingway] was a perfectionist, some things that he was not able to express to his satisfaction may prove to be of greater interest (to future biographers and students of literature if not to the general reading public) than certain of his second-best stories already published . . . But the evaluation of posthumous literary material requires above all an objective mind or, better still, a number of objective minds . . . All of his work may be confidently entrusted to the world for that general delight and edification which he intended and for which he labored, tiring himself to death.[7]

Fortunately, these manuscripts have, in one iteration or another, made their way into print: *A Moveable Feast* (edited by Mary Hemingway and Harry Brague, 1964); *Islands in the Stream* (edited by Mary Hemingway and Charles Scribner IV, 1970); *The Complete*

Poems (edited by Nicholas Gerogiannis, 1979, revised 1992); *The Dangerous Summer* (1985); *The Garden of Eden* (edited with extensive cuts by Tom Jenks, 1986); *True at First Light* (edited by Patrick Hemingway, 1999); *Under Kilimanjaro* (a scholarly edition of *True at First Light*, edited by Robert W. Lewis and Robert E. Fleming, 2005); and *A Moveable Feast: The Restored Edition* (edited by Seán Hemingway, 2009). The archival materials from which these works are drawn have been housed since 1972 in the Ernest Hemingway Collection at the John F. Kennedy Presidential Library in Boston, Massachusetts, and are open to scholars.

The first three volumes of a comprehensive collection of Hemingway's known correspondence, *The Letters of Ernest Hemingway*, were published in 2011, 2013 and 2015; a total of at least seventeen volumes is projected. Memoirs and biographies were published in rapid succession following Hemingway's death, most notably Carlos Baker's *Hemingway: A Life Story* of 1969, the official biography authorized by Mary; other offerings included the pulpy *Hemingway: Life and Death of a Giant*, which went to press while the dirt was still settling over Hemingway's grave. Half a century after his death, references and allusions to Hemingway continue to show up in just about every form of popular media, from graphic novels (Alison Bechdel's tragicomic graphic memoir *Fun Home* of 2006) and television series (the drama series *Mad Men*), to video games (*World of Warcraft*, a massive, multiplayer online role-playing game) and commercial products (including a luxury fountain pen, rum and an editing app). Hemingway has turned up as a character in a wide array of films and fiction, such as Woody Allen's *Midnight in Paris* (2011). On the campaign trail in 2008, then-future u.s. president Barack Obama told *Rolling Stone* magazine that *For Whom the Bell Tolls* was a favourite book. Hemingway remains widely taught in high school and college curricula, and his influence on letters is still detectable in the work of contemporary authors. 'A man can be destroyed but not defeated', Santiago says in *The Old Man and the Sea*.[8] Undefeated, Ernest Hemingway lives on.

References

Prologue

1 Ernest Hemingway, *A Farewell to Arms* (New York, 1995), pp. 320, 327.
2 Ernest Hemingway, *The Complete Short Stories of Ernest Hemingway: The Finca Vigía Edition* (New York, 1987), p. 291.

1 The Doctor and the Doctor's Wife, 1899–1919

1 Carlos Baker, *Ernest Hemingway: A Life Story* (New York, 1969), pp. 4–5. The scrapbooks Grace put together for Ernest are part of the Hemingway Collection at the John F. Kennedy Presidential Library in Boston. Digital copies are available for browsing at jfklibrary.org.
2 Susan F. Beegel, 'The Environment', in *Hemingway in Context*, eds Debra A. Moddelmog and Suzanne del Gizzo (New York, 2013), pp. 237–46; National Park Service, 'The Life of Theodore Roosevelt', www.nps.gov, 5 May 2015.
3 Sandra Spanier and Robert W. Trogdon, eds, *The Letters of Ernest Hemingway*, vol. I: *1907–1922* (New York, 2011), p. 10.
4 Miriam B. Mandel, *A Companion to Hemingway's 'Death in the Afternoon'* (Rochester, NY, 2004), p. 4.
5 For the porcupine incident, see Baker, *Life Story*, p. 16; for the heron incident, see Michael Reynolds, *The Young Hemingway* (New York, 1986), p. 71; for the boxing, see Spanier and Trogdon, eds, *Letters*, vol. I, p. 27.
6 Spanier and Trogdon, eds, *Letters*, vol. I, p. 14.
7 Ernest Hemingway, *The Complete Short Stories of Ernest Hemingway: The Finca Vigía Edition* (New York, 1987), p. 516. This work in progress was

never finished; it was first published, posthumously, in 1972.

8   For a discussion of Hemingway's religious practices, see H. R.
    Stoneback, 'In the Nominal Country of the Bogus: Hemingway's
    Catholicism and the Biographies', in *Hemingway: Essays of
    Reassessment*, ed. Frank Scafella (Oxford, 1991).

9   Hemingway, *Complete Short Stories*, p. 514.

10 Spanier and Trogdon, eds, *Letters*, vol. I, p. 27.

11 Michael Reynolds, *Young Hemingway*, p. 138.

12 Baker, *Life Story*, p. 72.

13 Ibid., p. 73.

14 Spanier and Trogdon, eds, *Letters*, vol. I, p. 40.

15 Hemingway, *Complete Short Stories*, p. 278.

16 Quoted in Jeffrey Meyers, *Ernest Hemingway: A Biography* (New York,
    1985), p. 212.

17 Hemingway, *Complete Short Stories*, p. 517.

18 Meyers, *Ernest Hemingway*, pp. 22–3.

19 Ibid.; Steve Paul, 'Annotation Added to Hemingway History', *Kansas
    City Star* (4 July 1999), p. J7.

20 Spanier and Trogdon, eds, *Letters*, vol. I, p. 55; John Fenstermaker,
    'Ernest Hemingway, 1917–1918: First Work, First War', in *War + Ink:
    New Perspectives on Ernest Hemingway's Early Life and Writings*, ed. Steve
    Paul, Gail Sinclair and Steven Trout (Kent, OH, 2014), p. 14.

21 Steve Paul, 'Hemingway's Kansas City: A Short Story', *Kansas City Star*
    (27 June 1999; updated 24 February 2015 online edn).

22 'The Star Copy Style', *Kansas City Star* (facs. *c.* 1915, reprod. 2006),
    collection of the author. A reproduction is available online from the
    Star, www.kansascity.com.

23 Quoted in Baker, *Life Story*, p. 187. These quotations are in response to
    reviews of *Men Without Women*. See Lee Wilson Dodd, *Saturday Review
    of Literature*, IV (19 November 1927), p. 322; and Joseph Wood Krutch,
    The Nation, CXXV (16 November 1927), p. 548.

24 Ernest Hemingway, 'At the End of the Ambulance Run', *Kansas City
    Star* (20 January 1918), p. 7C, repr. in Matthew J. Bruccoli, ed., *Ernest
    Hemingway, Cub Reporter* (Pittsburgh, PA, 1970), p. 33.

25 Spanier and Trogdon, eds, *Letters*, vol. I, p. 79.

26 Ibid., p. 80.

27 Ibid., p. 93.

28 'Would "Treat 'em Rough"' (18 April 1918), p. 4, in Bruccoli, ed., *Cub Reporter*, p. 51.

29 Spanier and Trogdon, eds, *Letters*, vol. i, pp. 71, 88 n. 6.

30 Ibid., pp. 58 n. 2, 61, 68–9.

31 Ibid., p. 59.

32 Ibid., p. 74.

33 Steve Paul, "'Drive', He Said": How Ted Brumback Helped Steer Ernest Hemingway into War and Writing', *Hemingway Review*, xxvii/1 (Fall 2007), pp. 21–38.

34 Spanier and Trogdon, eds, *Letters*, vol. i, p. 87.

35 Ernest Hemingway, 'Go Together from the Star to the Italian Front', *Kansas City Star* (13 May 1918), p. 4.

36 For a note resolving questions about the exact date of Hemingway's embarkation, see Steven Florczyk, *Hemingway, the Red Cross, and the Great War* (Kent, oh, 2014), pp. 152–3 n. 113.

37 Ibid., p. 41.

38 Spanier and Trogdon, eds, *Letters*, vol. i, pp. 111–12.

39 Ibid., p. 112.

40 Baker, *Life Story*, p. 42.

41 Ernest Hemingway, *A Farewell to Arms* (New York, 1995), p. 54.

42 Florczyk, *Hemingway, the Red Cross*, pp. 79–82.

43 Ibid., p. 79.

44 Spanier and Trogdon, eds, *Letters*, vol. i, p. 116.

45 Ibid., pp. 118, 120.

46 Ibid., p. 124.

47 Ibid., pp. 140–41, 127–8.

48 Ibid., pp. 145–6.

49 Ibid., pp. 157–8.

50 Henry S. Villard and James Nagel, *Hemingway in Love and War* (London, 1997), p. 279 n. 56.

51 Susan F. Beegel, 'Love in the Time of Influenza: Hemingway and the 1918 Pandemic', in *War + Ink*, ed. Paul, Sinclair and Trout, p. 36; Spanier and Trogdon, eds, *Letters*, vol. i, p. 147.

52 Baker, *Life Story*, pp. 52–3.

53 Ulrich Trumpener, 'Vittorio Veneto Campaign, 1918', in *The European Powers in the First World War: An Encyclopedia*, ed. Spencer C. Tucker (New York, 2013), pp. 726–7.

54 Spanier and Trogdon, eds, *Letters*, vol. I, p. 152.

55 Ibid., p. 162.

2 The Age Demanded, 1919–22

1 Sandra Spanier and Robert W. Trogdon, eds, *The Letters of Ernest Hemingway*, vol. I: *1907–1922* (New York, 2011), pp. 167, 169.

2 Ibid., p. 169; Carlos Baker, *Ernest Hemingway: A Life Story* (New York, 1969), p. 57.

3 Ibid., p. 58.

4 Spanier and Trogdon, eds, *Letters*, vol. I, p. 169.

5 Ibid., p. 177.

6 Henry S. Villard and James Nagel, *Hemingway in Love and War* (London, 1997), p. 163.

7 Ibid., pp. 163–4.

8 'Ag' would be changed to 'Luz' when Scribner's brought out a new edition in 1930; Paul Smith, *A Reader's Guide to the Short Stories of Ernest Hemingway* (Boston, MA, 1989), p. 26.

9 Villard and Nagel, *Love and War*, p. 163.

10 Ernest Hemingway, *The Complete Short Stories of Ernest Hemingway: The Finca Vigía Edition* (New York, 1987), p. 108.

11 Villard and Nagel, *Love and War*, p. 42.

12 Ibid., p. 162.

13 Michael Reynolds, *Hemingway's First War* (Princeton, NJ, 1976), p. 204.

14 Ernest Hemingway, *The Sun Also Rises* (New York, 2003), p. 120.

15 Spanier and Trogdon, eds, *Letters*, vol. I, p. 193.

16 Villard and Nagel, *Love and War*, pp. 164–8.

17 Hemingway, *Complete Short Stories*, p. 48.

18 Meyer Mathis, Letter to Mike Murphy (8 August 1957), Special Collections and Archive, Knox College Library, Galesburg, Illinois.

19 Villard and Nagel, *Love and War*, p. 39.

20 Spanier and Trogdon, eds, *Letters*, vol. I, p. 182.

21 See Steven Trout, '"Where Do We Go From Here?": Ernest Hemingway's "Soldier's Home" and American Veterans of World War I', *Hemingway Review*, XX/1 (Fall 2000), pp. 5–21.

22 Hemingway, *A Farewell to Arms* (New York, 1995), p. 63.

23 Spanier and Trogdon, eds, *Letters*, vol. I, pp. 185, 187; Hemingway, *Complete Short Stories*, p. 116.

24 Baker, *Life Story*, pp. 66–7.

25 Spanier and Trogdon, eds, *Letters*, vol. I, p. 227; Baker, *Life Story*, p. 68.

26 Spanier and Trogdon, eds, *Letters*, vol. I, p. 239.

27 Ibid., p. 256.

28 H. L. Mencken, *Chicago American* (28 June 1919), repr. in Ray Lewis White, 'Mencken's Lost Review of Winesburg, Ohio', *Notes on Modern American Literature* (Spring 1978).

29 Spanier and Trogdon, eds, *Letters*, vol. I, pp. 249, 258.

30 Bernice Kert, *The Hemingway Women* (New York, 1983), pp. 94–5.

31 Spanier and Trogdon, eds, *Letters*, vol. I, pp. 291–2 n. 3.

32 Hemingway, *Complete Short Stories*, p. 375.

33 Philip H. Melling, 'Memorial Landscapes', in *Hemingway and Africa*, ed. Miriam B. Mandel (Rochester, NY, 2011), p. 257; Kert, *Hemingway Women*, p. 103.

34 Quoted in Sylvia Beach, *Shakespeare and Company* (New York, 1959), p. 77.

35 For Stein as a popular writer, see Karen Leick, 'Popular Modernism: Little Magazines and the American Daily Press', *PMLA*, CXXIII/1 (January 2008), pp. 125–39. For Stein's psychological research, see Leon M. Solomons and Gertrude Stein, 'Normal Motor Automatism', *Psychological Review*, III (1896), pp. 492–512.

36 Sherwood Anderson, 'The Work of Gertrude Stein', *The Little Review* (Spring 1922); repr. in *Dictionary of Literary Biography: American Expatriate Writers: Paris in the Twenties*, Documentary Series XV, ed. Matthew J. Bruccoli and Robert W. Trogdon (Detroit, MI, 1997), pp. 12–13.

37 Beach, *Shakespeare and Company*, p. 77.

38 Ernest Hemingway, *A Moveable Feast: Restored Edition* (New York, 2009), p. 31.

39 Beach, *Shakespeare and Company*, pp. 78–9.

40 Ibid., p. 78.

41 Ibid., p. 81.

42 Spanier and Trogdon, eds, *Letters*, vol. I, pp. 313–14.

43 Hemingway, *A Moveable Feast: Restored*, p. 65.

44 Ibid., p. 73.

45 See Susan Beegel, *Hemingway's Craft of Omission: Four Manuscript Examples* (Ann Arbor, MI, 1988).

46 Hemingway, *A Moveable Feast: Restored*, p. 71.

47 Verna Kale, 'Hemingway's Poetry and the Paris Apprenticeship', *Hemingway Review*, XXVI/2 (Spring 2007), pp. 58–73.

48 Sandra Spanier et al., eds, *The Letters of Ernest Hemingway*, vol. II: *1923–1925* (New York, 2013), pp. 6–7. (Speculation on the date of conception is based on John Hemingway's 10 October birthday and a typical 40-week gestation.)

49 Hemingway, *A Moveable Feast*: *Restored*, p. 70.

50 Gertrude Stein, *The Autobiography of Alice B. Toklas* (New York, 1933), p. 262.

3 In Another Country, 1922–5

1 Ernest Hemingway, 'American Bohemians in Paris', in *By-Line: Ernest Hemingway*, ed. William White (New York, 1998), pp. 23–5.

2 Ernest Hemingway, *A Moveable Feast: The Restored Edition* (New York, 2009), p. 169. See also Verna Kale, '*A Moveable Feast* or "A Miserable Time Actually: Ernest Hemingway, Kay Boyle, and Modernist Memoir', in *Ernest Hemingway and the Geography of Memory*, ed. Mark Cirino and Mark P. Ott (Kent, OH, 2010), p. 135.

3 Sandra Spanier and Robert Trogdon, eds, *The Letters of Ernest Hemingway*, vol. I: *1907–1923* (New York, 2011), p. 328.

4 Edward J. O'Brien, ed., *The Best Short Stories of 1923 and the Yearbook of the American Short Story* (Cambridge, MA, 1924).

5 Ernest Hemingway Collection, Manuscripts, Up in Michigan, MS60, Item 800, John F. Kennedy Presidential Library and Museum, Boston, MA.

6 Hemingway, *A Moveable Feast*: *Restored*, p. 71.

7 Paul Smith, *A Reader's Guide to the Short Stories of Ernest Hemingway*, (Boston, 1989), p. 20.

8 Paul Smith, '1924: Hemingway's Luggage and the Miraculous Year', in *The Cambridge Companion to Ernest Hemingway*, ed. Scott Donaldson (New York, 1996), p. 45; Hemingway, *A Moveable Feast: Restored*, p. 22.

9 Ernest Hemingway, *In Our Time* (New York, 1996), p. 29; George
   Cheatham, 'The World War I Battle of Mons in Hemingway's
   In Our Time Chapter III', *Hemingway Review*, XXVI/2 (Spring 2007),
   p. 54.
10 Cheatham, 'Battle of Mons', pp. 52–3.
11 Hemingway, *In Our Time*, p. 63.
12 For dating of 'Quai', see Smith, *A Reader's Guide*, pp. 180–90.
13 Hemingway, *In Our Time*, p. 13.
14 See Matthew Stewart, 'It Was All a Pleasant Business: The Historical
   Context of "On the Quai at Smyrna"', XXIII/1 (Fall 2003), pp. 58–71.
15 See Michael Reynolds, *The Young Hemingway* (New York, 1986),
   pp. 71–2, 194.
16 Hemingway, *In Our Time*, p. 12.
17 Ernest Hemingway, 'Wanderings', *Poetry: A Magazine of Verse*, XXI/4
   (January 1923), p. 193.
18 Sandra Spanier et. al., eds, *The Letters of Ernest Hemingway*, vol. II:
   1923–1925 (New York, 2013), p. 41.
19 Ibid., p. 4.
20 Michael Reynolds, *Hemingway: The Paris Years* (New York, 1989), p. 79;
   Spanier et al., eds, *Letters*, vol. II, p. 4.
21 Spanier et al., eds, *Letters*, vol. II, p. 45.
22 Ibid., p. 91.
23 Carlos Baker, *Hemingway: The Writer as Artist*, 4th edn (New York,
   1972), p. 135. See also Paul Smith, *Reader's Guide*, p. 207. For 'fertility'
   and 'virility tales', see Hilary K. Justice, *The Bones of the Others* (Kent,
   OH, 2006), p. 6.
24 Ernest Hemingway, *The Complete Short Stories of Ernest Hemingway:
   The Finca Vigía Edition* (New York, 1987), p. 73.
25 Robert Trogdon, *The Lousy Racket: Hemingway, Scribners, and the
   Business of Literature* (Kent, OH, 2007), p. 5.
26 Hemingway, *In Our Time*, p. 85.
27 Smith, *Reader's Guide*, p. 76.
28 Matthew J. Bruccoli, ed., *The Only Thing That Counts: The Ernest
   Hemingway–Maxwell Perkins Correspondence* (Columbia, SC, 1996),
   pp. 202–3.
29 Ernest Hemingway, 'On Writing', in *The Nick Adams Stories* (New York,
   1999), pp. 237–8.

30 Paul Smith notes that the manuscript of 'Now I Lay Me' is the sole example in Hemingway's body of work in which Nick is first called 'Ernie', p. 173.

31 Hemingway, preface to *A Moveable Feast* (New York, 1964). See also Ernest Hemingway Collection, A Moveable Feast MS26, Manuscripts, John F. Kennedy Presidential Library and Museum, Boston, MA.

32 Carlos Baker, *Ernest Hemingway: A Life Story* (New York, 1969), p. 540.

4 The End of Something, 1925–6

1 Edmund Wilson, 'Mr Hemingway's Dry-Points', *The Dial* (October 1924), pp. 340–41.

2 Quoted in Robert W. Trogdon, *The Lousy Racket: Hemingway, Scribners, and the Business of Literature* (Kent, OH, 2007), p. 13.

3 Trogdon, *Lousy*, p. 15.

4 Sandra Spanier et al., eds, *The Letters of Ernest Hemingway*, vol. II: *1923–1925* (New York, 2013), p. 272.

5 Ibid., p. 318.

6 See Tom Dardis, *Firebrand: The Life of Horace Liveright* (New York, 1995), pp. 45–72.

7 Quoted ibid., p. 105.

8 Sandra Spanier et al., *Letters*, vol. II, p. 318.

9 Ernest Hemingway, 'Bull-Fighting: A Tragedy', *The Toronto Star Weekly* (20 October 1923); repr. in *By-Line: Ernest Hemingway*, ed. William White (New York, 1998), p. 95.

10 Ernest Hemingway, *The Sun Also Rises* (New York, 2003), p. 251.

11 Ibid., p. 38.

12 Ibid., p. 188.

13 Carol Acton, 'Diverting the Gaze: The Unseen Text in Women's War Writing', *College Literature*, XXXI/2 (2004), p. 57.

14 Ibid.

15 Hemingway, *Sun*, p. 247.

16 Ibid., p. 11.

17 Ibid.

18 See Jeremy Kaye, 'The "Whine" of Jewish Manhood: Re-Reading Hemingway's Anti-Semitism, Reimagining Robert Cohn', *Hemingway*

Review, xxv/2 (2006), pp. 44–60; and Jacob Michael Leland, 'Yes, That Is a Roll of Bills in My Pocket: The Economy of Masculinity in *The Sun Also Rises*', *Hemingway Review*, xxxvii/2 (2004), pp. 37–46.

19 Hemingway, *Sun*, p. 30.

20 See Ernest Hemingway, *The Sun Also Rises*, ed. Matthew J. Bruccoli (facs. edn, Detroit, mi, 1990).

21 Quoted in Trogdon, *Lousy*, p. 16.

22 The physical letter is held in *The Little Review* records, 1914–64, The University of Wisconsin-Milwaukee Libraries, Milwaukee, wi.

23 Trogdon, *Lousy*, pp. 19–20.

24 Dardis, *Firebrand*, p. 255.

25 Ibid., p. 256; Dardis rounds the 1,335 copies down to 1,300. For the exact publication details, see Audre Hanneman, *Ernest Hemingway: A Comprehensive Bibliography* (Princeton, nj, 1967), p. 7.

26 Charles Egleston, ed., *The House of Boni & Liveright, 1917–1933: A Documentary Volume*, Dictionary of Literary Biography, cclxxxviii (Detroit, mi, 2004), p. 337.

27 Louis Kronenberger, *Saturday Review of Literature*, xi (13 February 1926), quoted in Egleston, *Boni & Liveright*, p. 345.

28 Egleston, *Boni & Liveright*, p. 342.

29 Quoted in Dardis, *Firebrand*, p. 101.

30 Catherine Turner, *Marketing Modernism: Between the Two World Wars* (Amherst, ma, 2003), p. 9.

31 Spanier et al., eds, *Letters*, vol. ii, p. 295.

32 Ibid., pp. 434–6.

33 Ibid., p. 459.

34 See Andreas Huyssen, *After the Great Divide: Modernism, Mass Culture, Postmodernism* (Bloomington, in, 1986); Lawrence Rainey, *Institutions of Modernism: Literary Elites and Public Cultures* (New Haven, ct, 1998), p. 8.

35 Turner, *Marketing Modernism*, p. 3.

36 Scribner's, *Supplement to List of Spring Publications* (1926), quoted in Trogdon, *Lousy*, pp. 33–4.

37 Carlos Baker, *Ernest Hemingway: Selected Letters* (New York, 1981), p. 191.

38 Ernest Hemingway, *A Moveable Feast: The Restored Edition* (New York, 2009), pp. 119, 123.

39 Ibid., p. 231.

40 Ernest Hemingway, Letters to His Family, RBM 6189, Rare Books and Manuscripts, Special Collections Library, Pennsylvania State University, University Park, PA.

41 Ernest Hemingway, *The Complete Short Stories of Ernest Hemingway: The Finca Vigía Edition* (New York, 1987), p. 261.

42 Ibid., p. 258.

43 Quoted in James Mellow, *Hemingway: A Life Without Consequences* (Boston, MA, 1992), p. 343.

5 The Light of the World, 1926–9

1 Bernice Kert, *The Hemingway Women* (New York, 1983), pp. 183–9.

2 John Dos Passos, 'A Lost Generation', *New Masses*, II (December 1926), p. 26.

3 Unsigned but attributed to Fanny Butcher, 'Hemingway Seems Out of Focus in "The Sun Also Rises"', *Chicago Daily Tribune* (27 November 1926), ProQuest Historical Newspapers: *Chicago Tribune* (1849–1989), p. 13.

4 Quoted in Michael Reynolds, *Hemingway: The Homecoming* (New York, 1999), p. 92.

5 Robert W. Trogdon, ed., *Ernest Hemingway: A Literary Reference* (New York, 1999), p. 78.

6 Ibid.

7 Ibid.

8 Robert W. Trogdon, *The Lousy Racket: Hemingway, Scribners, and the Business of Literature* (Kent, OH, 2007), pp. 40–41.

9 Quoted ibid., pp. 47–8.

10 Daniel G. Tracy, 'Investing in Modernism: Smart Magazines, Parody, and Middlebrow Professional Judgment', *Journal of Modern Periodical Studies*, I/1 (2010), pp. 38–63.

11 Catherine Turner, *Marketing Modernism Between the Two World Wars* (Amherst, MA, 2003), p. 24.

12 Quoted in Matthew J. Bruccoli, ed., *The Only Thing That Counts: The Ernest Hemingway–Maxwell Perkins Correspondence* (New York, 1996), p. 188.

13 Trogdon, *Lousy*, pp. 45–6.

14 Matthew J. Bruccoli, ed., *Hemingway and the Mechanism of Fame* (Columbia, SC, 2006), pp. xviii–xix.

15 Matthew J. Bruccoli, *Fitzgerald and Hemingway: A Dangerous Friendship* (New York, 1994), p. 132.

16 Ernest Hemingway, *The Complete Short Stories of Ernest Hemingway: The Finca Vigía Edition* (New York, 1987), p. 212.

17 Quoted in Hilary K. Justice, '"Well, Well, Well": Cross-Gendered Autobiography and the Manuscript of "Hills Like White Elephants"', *Hemingway Review*, XVIII/1 (Fall 1998), p. 17.

18 Ibid., pp. 17–32; see also Carlos Baker, ed., *Ernest Hemingway: Selected Letters* (New York, 1981), p. 222.

19 Bruccoli, ed., *Only Thing*, p. 188.

20 Trogdon, *Literary Reference*, p. 88.

21 Ibid., p. 86.

22 Ernest Hemingway, *A Moveable Feast: The Restored Edition* (New York, 2009), p. 17.

23 Quoted in Trogdon, *Literary Reference*, p. 91.

24 Carlos Baker, *Ernest Hemingway: A Life Story* (New York, 1969), p. 187.

25 Reynolds, *Homecoming*, p. 167.

26 Baker, *Life Story*, p. 191.

27 Baker, ed., *Selected Letters*, p. 277.

28 Ibid., p. 280.

29 Ibid.

30 Quoted in Kert, *Hemingway Women*, p. 211.

31 Judith Fetterley, *The Resisting Reader* (Bloomington, IN, 1978), p. 71.

32 Ernest Hemingway, *A Farewell to Arms* (New York, 1995), p. 320.

33 Ibid., p. 327.

34 Quoted in Michael Reynolds, *Hemingway's First War: The Making of 'A Farewell to Arms'* (Princeton, NJ, 1976), p. 41.

35 Hemingway, *Farewell*, p. 185.

36 Ibid., p. 108.

37 Reynolds, *Homecoming*, pp. 207–8.

38 Malcolm Cowley, 'Not Yet Demobilized', *New York Herald Tribune Books*, XI/3 (6 October 1929), p. 1.

39 Trogdon, *Lousy*, pp. 68–9.

40 Bruccoli, *Dangerous Friendship*, pp. 111–15.

41 Ibid., p. 115.

42 'The Art of Fiction, XXI: Ernest Hemingway', *Paris Review*, V (Spring 1958); repr. in Trogdon, *Literary Reference*, p. 300.

43 Reynolds, *First War*, p. 49.

44 Ibid., p. 50.

45 Hemingway, *Farewell*, p. 332.

46 Bruccoli, ed., *Only Thing*, p. 91.

47 Baker, ed., *Selected Letters*, p. 297.

48 Bruccoli, ed., *Only Thing*, pp. 103–5.

49 Scott Donaldson, 'Censorship and *A Farewell to Arms*', *Studies in American Fiction*, XIX/1 (1991), pp. 88–9.

50 Trogdon, *Lousy*, p. 85.

51 Ibid., pp. 87, 91.

52 Fanny Butcher, 'Here is Genius, Critic Declares of Hemingway "A Farewell to Arms" Hailed as Great', *Chicago Daily Tribune* (28 September 1929), ProQuest Historical Newspapers: *Chicago Tribune* (1849–1989), p. 11.

53 Cowley, 'Not Yet Demobilized', pp. 1, 16.

54 Kiki (Alice Prin), introduction to *Kiki of Montparnasse* (New York, 1929), pp. 11–12.

55 Verna Kale, 'Hemingway's Poetry and the Paris Apprenticeship', *Hemingway Review*, XXVI/2 (Spring 2007), p. 69.

6 Shootism versus Sport, 1929–35

1 Archibald MacLeish, *Actfive and Other Poems* (New York, 1948), p. 53.

2 Ernest Hemingway, 'Statement on Writing', in *Modern Writers at Work*, ed. Josephine K. Piercy (New York, 1930), pp. 488–90; quoted in *Hemingway and the Mechanism of Fame*, ed. Matthew J. Bruccoli (Columbia, SC, 2006), p. 19.

3 Robert W. Trogdon, 'The Composition, Revision, Publication, and Reception of *Death in the Afternoon*', in *A Companion to Hemingway's 'Death in the Afternoon'*, ed. Miriam B. Mandel (New York, 2004), p. 30.

4 Ernest Hemingway, *Death in the Afternoon* (New York, 1996), p. 51.

5 Mandel, ed., *Companion*, p. 8.

6 See Peter Messent, '"The Real Thing?": Representing the Bullfight and Spain in *Death in the Afternoon*', in *Companion*, ed. Mandel, p. 127. As

Messent notes, 'translation of one culture for the understanding of another can never be a neutral process'.

7 Hemingway, *Death*, p. 2.

8 Ibid., p. 135.

9 Linda Wagner-Martin, '"I Like You Less and Less": The Stein Subtext in *Death in the Afternoon*', in *Companion*, ed. Mandel, p. 64.

10 Ibid., pp. 68–9; Hemingway, *Death*, p. 190.

11 Hemingway, *Death*, p. 191.

12 F. Scott Fitzgerald, 'The Rich Boy', in *Babylon Revisited and Other Stories* (New York, 2003), p. 152.

13 Hemingway, *Death*, p. 191.

14 Hilary K. Justice, '"Prejudiced through Experience": *Death in the Afternoon* and the Problem of Authorship', in *Companion*, ed. Mandel, p. 250.

15 Hemingway, *Death*, p. 192.

16 Carlos Baker, ed., *Ernest Hemingway: Selected Letters* (New York, 1981), p. 346.

17 Michael Reynolds, *Hemingway: The 1930s* (New York, 1997), pp. 57–8, 77.

18 Edmund Wilson, Introduction to *In Our Time* (New York, 1930), pp. x–xi.

19 See Trogdon, 'Composition', in *Companion*, ed. Mandel, pp. 36–7.

20 Quoted in Robert W. Trogdon, ed., *Ernest Hemingway: A Literary Reference* (New York, 1999), p. 129.

21 Baker, ed., *Selected Letters*, p. 369.

22 Max Eastman, 'Bull in the Afternoon', *New Republic* (7 June 1933), pp. 94–7.

23 See Trogdon, *Literary Reference*, p. 137.

24 Anonymous, 'Hemingway Slaps Eastman in Face', *New York Times* (14 August 1937), p. 15.

25 Sandra Spanier et al., eds, *The Letters of Ernest Hemingway*, vol. II: *1923–1925* (New York, 2013), pp. 191–5; Constantin Alajalov, 'Vanity Fair's Own Paper Dolls – no. 5', *Vanity Fair* (March 1934), p. 29.

26 Robert W. Trogdon, *The Lousy Racket: Hemingway, Scribners, and the Business of Literature* (Kent, OH, 2007), p. 142.

27 Baker, ed., *Selected Letters*, p. 397.

28 Susan F. Beegel, ed., *Hemingway's Neglected Short Fiction: New Perspectives* (Ann Arbor, MI, 1989), p. 11.

29 A. E. Hotchner, *Papa Hemingway* (New York, 1966), p. 164.

30 Arthur Power, *Conversations with James Joyce*, ed. Clive Hart (New York, 1974), p. 107, quoted in David Kerner, 'The Ambiguity of "A Clean, Well-Lighted Place"', *Studies in Short Fiction*, XXIX/4 (1992), p. 561.

31 See Stan Ulanski, *The Billfish Story: Swordfish, Sailfish, Marlin, and Other Gladiators of the Sea* (Athens, GA, 2013), pp. 42–59; and Key West Administration, 'Fisherman's Paradise', *Key West in Transition: A Guide Book for Visitors* (Key West, FL, 1934).

32 Mark P. Ott, 'Fishing', in *Ernest Hemingway in Context*, ed. Debra Moddelmog and Suzanne del Gizzo (New York, 2013), pp. 250–51.

33 Ibid., p. 248.

34 Ernest Hemingway, 'On the Blue Water: A Gulf Stream Letter', in *Esquire* (April 1936); repr. in *By-Line: Ernest Hemingway*, ed. William White (New York, 1998), p. 237.

35 See Ernest Hemingway letter to Madelaine Hemingway (3 June 1935), Ernest Hemingway Letters to His Family, RBM 6189, Rare Books and Manuscripts, Special Collections Library, Pennsylvania State University, University Park, PA.

36 Bernice Kert, *The Hemingway Women* (New York, 1983), p. 250.

37 Silvio Calabi, 'Ernest Hemingway on Safari: The Game and the Guns', in *Hemingway and Africa*, ed. Miriam B. Mandel (Rochester, NY, 2011), p. 88.

38 James Brasch and Joseph Sigman, *Hemingway's Library: A Composite Record* (New York, 1981), p. 318.

39 Baker, ed., *Selected Letters*, pp. 402–3.

40 Ernest Hemingway, 'Monologue to the Maestro: A High Seas Letter', *Esquire* (October 1935), repr. in *By-Line*, ed. White, pp. 215–16.

41 Ernest Hemingway, *Green Hills of Africa* (New York, 2003), p. 27.

42 Quoted in Trogdon, *Lousy*, pp. 144–5.

43 Michael Reynolds, *Hemingway: The 1930s* (New York, 1997), p. 215.

44 Malcolm Cowley, 'Breakdown', *New Republic* (6 June 1934), p. 105.

45 Ernest Hemingway Collection, Arnold Gingrich, letter to Ernest Hemingway (4 August 1933), Box 52, John F. Kennedy Presidential Library and Museum, Boston, MA.

46 Kevin Maier, '"A Trick Men Learn in Paris": Hemingway, *Esquire*, and Mass Tourism', *Hemingway Review*, XXXI/2 (Spring 2012), p. 66.

47 Ernest Hemingway Collection, Arnold Gingrich, letter to Ernest Hemingway (20 June 1933), Box 52, John F. Kennedy Presidential Library and Museum, Boston, MA.

48 Ernest Hemingway, 'Marlin off the Morro: A Cuban Letter', in *By-Line*, ed. White, p. 140.
49 Ulanski, *Billfish Story*, p. 54.
50 Prosanta Chakrabarty, 'Papa's Fish: A Note on *Neomerinthe hemingwayi*', *Hemingway Review*, XXV/1 (Fall 2005), pp. 109–11.
51 Ulanski, *Billfish Story*, p. 52.
52 Ernest Hemingway, 'On the Blue Water: A Gulf Stream Letter', in *By-Line*, ed. White, p. 239.
53 Ulanski, *Billfish Story*, p. 52.

7 The Soul of Spain, 1935–9

1 Wyndham Lewis, 'The Dumb Ox', *Life and Letters* (April 1934), pp. 33–45; repr. in *Ernest Hemingway: The Critical Heritage*, ed. Jeffrey Meyers (London, 1982), p. 187.
2 Matthew J. Bruccoli, ed., *Hemingway and the Mechanism of Fame* (Columbia, SC, 2006), p. 43.
3 Alfred Kazin, 'Hemingway's First Book on His Own People', *New York Herald Tribune Books* (17 October 1937), p. 3.
4 Ibid.
5 Paul Dickson and Thomas B. Allen, *The Bonus Army: An American Epic* (New York, 2004), pp. 1–6, 115.
6 Ernest Hemingway, 'Who Murdered the Vets?', *New Masses*, XVI (17 September 1935), pp. 9–10.
7 Ibid.
8 Ibid.
9 Ivan Kashkin, 'Ernest Hemingway: A Tragedy of Craftsmanship', *International Literature*, V (May 1935), pp. 72–90, quoted in *Ernest Hemingway: A Literary Reference*, ed. Robert W. Trogdon (New York, 1999), pp. 167–8; Carlos Baker, ed., *Ernest Hemingway: Selected Letters* (New York, 1981), p. 419.
10 Baker, ed., *Selected Letters*, p. 419.
11 Quoted in Carlos Baker, *Ernest Hemingway: A Life Story* (New York, 1969), p. 288, see also p. 290.
12 Caroline Moorehead, *Gellhorn: A Twentieth-Century Life* (New York, 2004), p. 101.

13 Ernest Hemingway, *The Fifth Column and Four Stories of the Spanish Civil War* (New York, 1998), p. 66.

14 See Baker, *Life Story*, p. 297; Michael Reynolds, *Hemingway: The 1930s* (New York, 1997), pp. 243–4; Moorehead, *Gellhorn*, p. 101; and Carl Rollyson, *Beautiful Exile: The Life of Martha Gellhorn* (Lincoln, NE, 2007), p. 89. 'Ernest Hemingway Residence' is item #18 on the map included in *Key West in Transition: A Guide Book for Visitors* (Key West, FL, 1934).

15 Ernest Hemigway, 'The Sights of Whitehead Street: A Key West Letter', *Esquire* (April 1935), in *Ernest Hemingway*, ed. William White (New York, 1998), p. 192.

16 Lewis Gannett, 'Books 'n' Things', syndicated column, quoted in Bernice Kert, *The Hemingway Women* (New York, 1983), p. 289.

17 See Kert, *Hemingway Women*, pp. 248–9.

18 Quoted in Caroline Moorhead, ed., *Selected Letters of Martha Gellhorn* (New York, 2007), pp. 46–7.

19 Scott Donaldson, *Fitzgerald and Hemingway: Works and Days* (New York, 2009), p. 380.

20 Quoted in Moorhead, *Gellhorn*, p. 113; and Baker, *Life Story*, p. 304.

21 See Amanda Vaill, *Hotel Florida: Truth, Love, and Death in the Spanish Civil War* (New York, 2014); and Josephine Herbst, 'The Starched Blue Sky of Spain', *Noble Savage*, I (1960).

22 Martha Gellhorn, 'Only the Shells Whine', *Collier's* (17 July 1937), p. 13.

23 Herbst, 'Starched Blue Sky', p. 93.

24 Ibid (emphasis is Herbst's).

25 Vaill, *Hotel Florida*, p. 153.

26 Herbst, 'Starched Blue Sky', p. 80.

27 Baker, *Selected Letters*, p. 456.

28 Ibid., p. 458.

29 Ernest Hemingway, 'Notes on the Next War: A Serious Topical Letter', *Esquire* (September 1935), quoted in *By-Line: Ernest Hemingway*, ed. William White (New York, 1998), pp. 207, 212.

30 Ernest Hemingway, 'The Time Now, The Place Spain', *Ken* (7 April 1938), p. 37.

31 William Braasch Watson, 'Hemingway's Spanish Civil War Dispatches: Introduction', *Hemingway Review*, VII (Spring 1988), p. 5.

32 Alex Vernon, *Hemingway's Second War: Bearing Witness to the Spanish Civil War* (Iowa City, IA, 2011), pp. 53, 61.

33 Ernest Hemingway, Preface, *The Fifth Column and the First Forty-Nine Stories* (New York, 1939), p. vi.

34 Baker, ed., *Selected Letters*, p. 458.

35 Kert, *Hemingway Women*, p. 293.

36 Ernest Hemingway, 'Fascism is a Lie', *New Masses* (22 June 1937), p. 4.

37 Robert W. Trogdon, *The Lousy Racket: Hemingway, Scribners, and the Business of Literature* (Kent, OH, 2007), p. 172.

38 Bruccoli, *Mechanism*, p. xxiii.

39 Baker, ed., *Selected Letters*, p. 648.

40 Hemingway, Preface, *The Fifth Column and the First Forty-Nine*, p. vi.

41 Hemingway, *Fifth Column and Four Stories*, p. 78.

42 Verna Kale, 'Review of *The Fifth Column*', *Hemingway Review*, XXVII (Spring 2008), pp. 131–4.

43 Kert, *Hemingway Women*, p. 301.

8 Notes on the Next War, 1939–44

1 Carlos Baker, *Ernest Hemingway: A Life Story* (New York, 1969), pp. 339–40. Gellhorn joined Hemingway sometime between February and April 1939, with the earlier date likely more accurate. See Caroline Moorehead, *Gellhorn: A Twentieth-Century Life* (New York, 2004), p. 157.

2 Carlos Baker, ed., *Ernest Hemingway: Selected Letters* (New York, 1981), p. 483.

3 Ibid., p. 493.

4 Ibid., p. 499.

5 James Brasch and Joseph Sigman, *Hemingway's Library: A Composite Record* (New York, 1981), p. xxxix.

6 Caroline Moorehead, ed., *Selected Letters of Martha Gellhorn* (New York, 2007), p. 81.

7 'Glamor Girl', *Time* , XXXV/12 (18 March 1940), p. 92.

8 See Bernice Kert, *The Hemingway Women* (New York, 1983), pp. 289, 295; 'Glamor Girl', p. 92.

9 Moorehead, *Gellhorn*, p. 167.

10 'The Hemingways in Sun Valley: The Novelist Takes a Wife', *Life* (6 January 1941), pp. 50–51.

11 For a discussion of possible models for Robert Jordan, see Alex Vernon, *Hemingway's Second War: Bearing Witness to the Spanish Civil War* (Iowa City, IA, 2011), pp. 169–73.

12 'Hemingway's Spanish War', *Newsweek* (21 October 1940), p. 50; Amanda Vaill, *Hotel Florida: Truth, Love, and Death in the Spanish Civil War* (New York, 2014), pp. 246–7; Vernon, *Second War*, pp. 209–10.

13 Vernon, *Second War*, p. 199.

14 Ernest Hemingway, *For Whom the Bell Tolls* (New York, 1940). Hemingway likely used the *Oxford Book of English Prose* of 1925 as his source text. See John Donne, 'The Bell', in *The Oxford Book of English Prose* (Oxford, 1925), pp. 171–2.

15 Ralph Thompson, 'Books of the Times', *New York Times* (21 October 1940), p. 15.

16 Quoted in Robert W. Trogdon, *The Lousy Racket: Hemingway, Scribners, and the Business of Literature* (Kent, OH, 2007), p. 213.

17 Robert Trogdon, 'Money and Marriage: Self-Censorship in *For Whom the Bell Tolls*', *Hemingway Review*, XXII/2 (Spring 2003), p. 11.

18 Ibid., p. 15.

19 Trogdon, *Lousy*, p. 226.

20 Baker, ed., *Selected Letters*, p. 521.

21 Allen Josephs, *For Whom the Bell Tolls: Ernest Hemingway's Undiscovered Country* (New York, 1994), p. 131; and Vernon, *Second War*, p. 150.

22 Vernon, *Second War*, p. 153.

23 Alvah Bessie, 'Hemingway's "For Whom the Bell Tolls"', *New Masses* (5 November 1940), p. 25.

24 Josephs, *Undiscovered Country*, p. 20.

25 Bessie, 'Hemingway's', p. 25.

26 Quoted in Vernon, *Second War*, p. 145.

27 Quoted in Trogdon, *Lousy*, p. 201.

28 Jeffrey Meyers, *Hemingway: A Biography* (New York, 1985), p. 339.

29 Michael Reynolds, *Hemingway: The Final Years* (New York, 1999), p. 45.

30 Anthony E. Rebollo, 'The Taxation of Ernest Hemingway', *Hemingway Review*, XXVI/2 (Spring, 2007), pp. 31–2.

31 Baker, ed., *Selected Letters*, p. 525.

32 Ibid., pp. 525 and 529.

33 Ibid., p. 536.

34 Ibid., p. 537.

35 Ibid., p. 528.
36 Edmund Wilson, 'Ernest Hemingway: Bourdon Gauge of Morale', *Atlantic Monthly* (July 1939), p. 41.
37 Edmund Wilson, *The Wound and the Bow: Seven Studies in Literature* (Cambridge, 1941; new printing with corrections, New York, 1947), p. 242.
38 Martha Gellhorn, *Travels with Myself and Another* (New York, 1984), p. 30.
39 Ibid., p. 62.
40 Peter Moreira, *Hemingway on the China Front: His wwii Spy Mission with Martha Gellhorn* (Washington, DC, 2006), p. 19.
41 Gellhorn, *Travels*, p. 60.
42 Baker, ed., *Selected Letters*, pp. 531–2.
43 Ibid., p. 520.
44 Reynolds, *Hemingway: The Final Years*, p. 86.
45 Ernest Hemingway, ed., *Men at War: The Best War Stories of All Time* (New York, 1942), p. xi.
46 Reynolds, *Final Years*, pp. 56–8.
47 Ibid., pp. 65–6.
48 J. Edgar Hoover to R. G. Leddy (19 December 1942), quoted in Moreira, *China Front*, p. 195.
49 Moorehead, ed., *Selected Letters*, p. 131.
50 Kert, *Hemingway Women*, p. 375.
51 Moorehead, *Gellhorn*, p. 195.
52 Moorehcad, ed., *Selected Letters*, p. 159.
53 Kert, *Hemingway Women*, p. 391.

9 The Battler, 1944–7

1 Carlos Baker, *Ernest Hemingway: A Life Story* (New York, 1969), pp. 384–5.
2 Bernice Kert, *The Hemingway Women* (New York, 1983), p. 390.
3 Michael Reynolds, *Hemingway: The Final Years* (New York, 1999), pp. 84–5.
4 Peter Moreira, *Hemingway on the China Front: His wwii Spy Mission with Martha Gellhorn* (Washington, DC, 2006), pp. 195–6.

5 Reynolds, *Final Years*, pp. 88, 92.
6 See Sandra Spanier, 'Rivalry, Romance, and War Reporters: Martha Gellhorn's *Love Goes to Press* and the *Collier's* Files', in *Hemingway and Women: Female Critics and the Female Voice*, ed. Lawrence R. Broer and Gloria Holland (Tuscaloosa, AL, 2002).
7 Kert, *Hemingway Women*, p. 398.
8 Caroline Moorhead, ed., *Selected Letters of Martha Gellhorn* (New York, 2007), p. 426.
9 Quoted in Spanier, 'Rivalry', pp. 273–4.
10 Ernest Hemingway, 'Voyage to Victory', in *By-Line: Ernest Hemingway*, ed. William White (New York, 1998), p. 355.
11 See Robert Fuller, 'Hemingway at Rambouillet', *Hemingway Review*, XXXIII/2 (Spring 2014), pp. 66–80.
12 Quoted in Robert W. Trogdon, ed., *Ernest Hemingway: A Literary Reference* (New York, 1999), p. 259.
13 Ernest Hemingway, 'The Day We Drove Back from Nancy to Paris', Box 32 item 356A, Ernest Hemingway Collection, John F. Kennedy Presidential Library, Boston, MA.
14 Ernest Hemingway, 'Battle for Paris', in *By-Line*, ed. White, p. 365.
15 Fuller, 'Rambouillet', p. 78.
16 Carlos Baker, ed., *Ernest Hemingway: Selected Letters* (New York, 1981), p. 566.
17 Ibid., pp. 571–2.
18 Ibid., p. 576.
19 Ibid., pp. 580–81.
20 Ibid., p. 574.
21 This line appears in a draft of an unfinished, unpublished novel. Quoted in Michael Reynolds, *Hemingway: The Homecoming* (New York, 1999), p. 154.
22 Reynolds, *Final Years*, p. 140.
23 Ibid., pp. 343–4.
24 M. C. Tartaglia et al., 'Chronic Traumatic Encephalopathy and Other Neurodegenerative Proteinopathies', *Frontiers in Human Neuroscience*, VIII/30 (2014).
25 Brandon E. Gavett et al., 'Chronic Traumatic Encephalopathy: A Potential Late Effect of Sports-Related Concussive and Subconcussive Head Trauma', *Clinics in Sports Medicine*, XXX/1 (2011), p. 180.

26 Ibid.

27 Phillip Young, *Ernest Hemingway: A Reconsideration* (University Park, PA, 1966), p. 163.

28 Baker, *Life Story*, p. 405.

29 Reynolds, *Final Years*, pp. 131–2; quoted in Matthew J. Bruccoli, ed., *Hemingway and the Mechanism of Fame* (Columbia, SC, 2006), p. 109.

30 Mary Welsh Hemingway, *How It Was* (New York, 1976), pp. 177, 183–4.

31 Caroline Moorehead, *Gellhorn: A Twentieth-Century Life* (New York, 2004), p. 198; and Rose Marie Burwell, *Hemingway: The Postwar Years and the Posthumous Novels* (Cambridge, 1999), pp. 47–8.

32 Welsh Hemingway, *How It Was*, p. 187.

33 Ibid., p. 189.

34 Baker, ed., *Selected Letters*, p. 611.

35 Welsh Hemingway, *How It Was*, pp. 260–61.

36 Ernest Hemingway, *Islands in the Stream* (New York, 1970), p. 51.

37 Baker, ed., *Selected Letters*, pp. 604–5.

38 Ibid., p. 616.

39 Burwell, *Postwar Years*, p. 1.

40 Hemingway to Charles Lanham (12 June 1948), quoted in Burwell, *Postwar Years*, p. 97.

41 Hilary K. Justice, *The Bones of the Others: The Hemingway Text from the Lost Manuscripts to the Posthumous Novels* (Kent, OH, 2006), p. 3.

42 Quoted in Justice, *Bones*, p. 57.

43 See, for example, Baker, ed., *Selected Letters*, p. 396.

44 Quoted in Joseph Fruscione, *Faulkner and Hemingway: Biography of a Literary Rivalry* (Columbus, OH, 2012), p. 133.

45 Ibid., p. 134.

46 Reynolds, *Final*, p. 154.

47 Bruccoli, ed., *Mechanism*, p. 94.

10 The Tradesman's Return, 1947–51

1 Matthew J. Bruccoli, ed., *The Only Thing That Counts: The Ernest Hemingway-Maxwell Perkins Correspondence* (Columbia, SC, 1996), p. 345.

2 Robert W. Trogdon, *The Lousy Racket: Hemingway, Scribners, and the Business of Literature* (Kent, OH, 2007), p. 228.

3 Carlos Baker, ed., *Ernest Hemingway: Selected Letters* (New York, 1981), p. 632.

4 Ibid., p. 617.

5 See A. E. Hotchner, *The Day I Fired Alan Ladd and Other wwii Adventures* (Columbia, MO, 2002).

6 Michael Reynolds, *Hemingway: The Final Years* (New York, 1999), pp. 177–81.

7 Carlos Baker, *Ernest Hemingway: A Life Story* (New York, 1969), p. 469.

8 Carl P. Eby, *Hemingway's Fetishism: Psychoanalysis and the Mirror of Manhood* (Albany, NY, 1999), p. 19.

9 Bernice Kert, *The Hemingway Women* (New York, 1983), pp. 438–9.

10 Baker, *Life Story*, p. 471.

11 *Time*, 56 (11 September 1950), p. 110, quoted in Matthew J. Bruccoli, ed., *Hemingway and the Mechanism of Fame* (Columbia, SC, 2006), p. 106.

12 Baker, ed., *Selected Letters*, p. 660.

13 Ernest Hemingway, *Across the River and Into the Trees* (New York, 1996), pp. 84–7.

14 Ernest Hemingway, to Charles Scribner III (10 May 1950), Archives of Charles Scribner's Sons, Ernest Hemingway Collection, Series 10B, Box 774 Folder 2, Department of Rare Books and Special Collections, Princeton University Library, NJ.

15 Hemingway, *Across the River*, p. 195.

16 Ernest Hemingway, to Charles Scribner III (12 June 1948), Archives of Charles Scribner's Sons, Ernest Hemingway Collection, Series 10B, Box 774 Folder 1, Department of Rare Books and Special Collections, Princeton University Library, NJ.

17 Trogdon, *Lousy*, p. 230; Reynolds, *Final Years*, p. 184.

18 Mary Welsh Hemingway, *How It Was* (New York, 1976), p. 240.

19 Ibid., p. 178.

20 Ibid., p. 103.

21 Baker, ed., *Selected Letters*, p. 667.

22 Welsh Hemingway, *How It Was*, pp. 239–46.

23 Baker, ed., *Selected Letters*, p. 673.

24 Trogdon, *Lousy*, p. 232.

25 Ibid., p. 234.

26 Quoted in Robert W. Trogdon, ed., *Ernest Hemingway: A Literary Reference* (New York, 1999), pp. 280–83.

27 John O'Hara, 'The Author's Name Is Hemingway', *New York Times Book Review* (10 September 1950), p. 1.

28 Quoted in Baker, *Life Story*, p. 487.

29 Baker, ed., *Selected Letters*, p. 713.

30 Quoted in Trogdon, *Lousy*, p. 235.

31 Hemingway, *Across the River*, pp. 187, 215.

32 Ibid., pp. 137, 184, 213.

33 Ibid., pp. 16, 130.

34 Ibid., pp. 21, 37, 53.

35 Ibid., pp. 64, 107. The line is also an allusion to a poem by François Villon, famously translated into English by Dante Gabriel Rossetti. *Across the River and Into the Trees* is full of many other such literary allusions, in addition to the allusions to Hemingway's own work noted here.

36 Ibid., p. 117.

37 Ibid., p. 145.

38 Ibid., p. 196. See Michael Reynolds, *Hemingway's First War* (Princeton, NJ, 1976), p. 296.

39 Hemingway, *Across the River*, p. 246.

40 Ibid., pp. 168, 215; Ernest Hemingway, *The Complete Short Stories of Ernest Hemingway: The Finca Vigía Edition* (New York, 1987), p. 164.

41 Hemingway, *Across the River*, p. 283.

42 Ernest Hemingway, to Charles Scribner III (10 May 1950), Archives of Charles Scribner's Sons, Ernest Hemingway Collection, Series 10B, Box 774 Folder 2, Department of Rare Books and Special Collections, Princeton University Library, Princeton, NJ.

43 Quoted in Jeffrey Meyers, *Hemingway: A Biography* (New York, 1985), p. 459.

44 David Earle, *All Man! Hemingway, 1950s Men's Magazines, and the Masculine Persona* (Kent, OH, 2009), p. 18.

45 Ibid., p. 137.

46 N.B. The Nobel Prize in Literature for 1949 was awarded in 1950. See Joseph Fruscione, *Faulkner and Hemingway: Biography of a Literary Rivalry* (Columbus, OH, 2012), p. 156.

47 Quoted ibid., pp. 160–61.

48 Baker, ed., *Selected Letters*, p. 720.

49 Ibid., pp. 730–31.

50 Ibid., p. 698.

11 The Undefeated, 1951–4

1 Quoted in Jeffrey Meyers, *Hemingway: A Biography* (New York, 1985), p. 240.
2 Ernest Hemingway, letter to Madeleine Hemingway (3 June 1952), Ernest Hemingway Letters to His Family, RBM 6189, Rare Books and Manuscripts, Special Collections Library, Pennsylvania State University, University Park, PA.
3 John Hemingway, *Strange Tribe: A Family Memoir* (New Haven, CT, 2007), p. 113; Bernice Kert, *The Hemingway Women* (New York, 1983), p. 463.
4 Carlos Baker, ed., *Ernest Hemingway: Selected Letters* (New York, 1981), p. 762.
5 See Susan Beegel, 'Conclusion: The Critical Reputation of Ernest Hemingway', in *The Cambridge Companion to Ernest Hemingway*, ed. Scott Donaldson (New York, 1996), p. 275.
6 See Scott Donaldson, *Death of a Rebel: The Charlie Fenton Story* (Lanham, MD, 2012), Chapter Four.
7 Baker, ed., *Selected Letters*, p. 673.
8 Ernest Hemingway, 'On the Blue Water: A Gulf Stream Letter', in *Esquire* (April 1936), repr. in *By-Line: Ernest Hemingway*, ed. William White (New York, 1998), pp. 239–40.
9 Larry Grimes, 'Lions on the Beach: Dream, Place, and Memory in *The Old Man and the Sea*', in *Ernest Hemingway and the Geography of Memory*, ed. Mark Cirino and Mark P. Ott (Kent, OH, 2010), p. 58.
10 Baker, ed., *Selected Letters*, p. 738.
11 Carlos Baker, *Ernest Hemingway: A Life Story* (New York, 1969), p. 500.
12 Robert W. Trogdon, *The Lousy Racket: Hemingway, Scribners, and the Business of Literature* (Kent, OH, 2007), p. 250.
13 Quoted in Robert W. Trogdon, ed., *Ernest Hemingway: A Literary Reference* (New York, 1999), p. 285.
14 Baker, ed., *Selected Letters*, p. 821.
15 Michael Reynolds, *Hemingway: The Final Years* (New York, 1999), pp. 231–4.
16 See Sarah M. Buel, 'Fifty Obstacles to Leaving, a.k.a., Why Abuse Victims Stay', *Colorado Lawyer*, XXVIII/10 (October 1999), pp. 19–28, http://web.law.asu.edu, accessed 4 October 2015.
17 See Reynolds, *Final Years*, p. 272.

18 Ibid., pp. 264–7; Ernest Hemingway, *Under Kilimanjaro*, ed. Robert W. Lewis and Robert E. Fleming (Kent, OH, 2005), p. 2. See also Nghana Tamu Lewis, 'Race and Ethnicity: Africans', in *Ernest Hemingway in Context*, ed. Debra A. Moddelmog and Suzanne del Gizzo (Cambridge, 2013).

19 Hemingway, *Under Kilimanjaro*, pp. 8, 114.

20 Ibid., p. 388; Mary Welsh Hemingway, *How It Was* (New York, 1976), p. 368.

21 Hemingway, *Under Kilimanjaro*, pp. 335, 363.

22 Welsh Hemingway, *How It Was*, pp. 368–70.

23 Carl Eby, 'Hemingway, Tribal Law, and the Identity of the Widow in *True at First Light*', *Hemingway Review*, XXI/2 (Spring 2002), p. 150.

24 Reynolds, *Final Years*, pp. 270–71.

25 Hemingway, *Under Kilimanjaro*, pp. 23, 118.

26 Welsh Hemingway, *How It Was*, pp. 371–2; and Ernest Hemingway, 'The Christmas Gift', *Look* (20 April 1954 and 4 May 1954), repr. in *By-Line: Ernest Hemingway*, ed. William White (New York, 1998), pp. 432–3.

27 Welsh Hemingway, *How It Was*, pp. 384–5.

28 Reynolds, *Final Years*, p. 274.

29 The United Press, 'Hemingway Out of the Jungle; Arm Hurt, He Says Luck Holds', *New York Times* (26 January 1954), p. 1.

30 See, for example, UPA and The Times of India News Service, 'Hemingway Dies in Accident', *Times of India* (25 January 1954), p. 1.

31 'News Summary & Index', *New York Times* (25 January 1954), p. 20.

32 Ernest Hemingway, in *By-Line*, ed. White, p. 469.

33 Ernest Hemingway Collection, manuscript fragment [*c.* 1931], Box 43 item 767C, John F. Kennedy Presidential Library and Museum, Boston, MA; Welsh Hemingway, *How It Was*, p. 389.

12 The Last Good Country, 1954–61

1 Mary Welsh Hemingway, *How It Was* (New York, 1976), p. 390.

2 Ernest Hemingway, 'The Christmas Gift', *Look* (20 April 1954 and 4 May 1954), repr. in *By-Line: Ernest Hemingway*, ed. William White (New York, 1998), p. 450; Carlos Baker, ed., *Ernest Hemingway: Selected Letters* (New York, 1981), p. 828.

3 Welsh Hemingway, *How It Was*, p. 400.

4 Quoted in Robert W. Trogdon, ed., *Ernest Hemingway: A Literary Reference* (New York, 1999), p. 297.

5 Bickford Sylvester, 'The Cuban Context of *The Old Man and the Sea*', in *The Cambridge Companion to Ernest Hemingway*, ed. Scott Donaldson (New York, 1996), pp. 252–3; Ernest Hemingway, *The Old Man and the Sea* (New York, 1995), p. 9.

6 Michael Reynolds, *Hemingway: The Final Years* (New York, 1999), pp. 293–6.

7 Rose Marie Burwell, *Hemingway: The Postwar Years and the Posthumous Novels* (Cambridge, 1999), pp. 150–52.

8 Reynolds, *Final Years*, pp. 300–301.

9 Michael Reynolds, *Hemingway: The Paris Years* (New York, 1989), p. 106.

10 Welsh Hemingway, *How It Was*, p. 446.

11 Reynolds, *Final Years*, p. 260.

12 Baker, ed., *Selected Letters*, p. 882.

13 Reynolds, *Final Years*, p. 307.

14 Baker, ed., *Selected Letters*, pp. 884, 888.

15 Ibid., p. 892.

16 Ernest Hemingway, *A Moveable Feast: The Restored Edition* (New York, 2009), p. 234.

17 For an overview of the social and cultural shifts during the 1950s, see William H. Young and Nancy K. Young, *The 1950s* (Greenwood, CT, 2004).

18 Seán Hemingway, ed., Introduction to *Hemingway on War* (New York, 2003), p. xxviii.

19 Reynolds, *Final Years*, p. 321.

20 'The Hero of the Code', *Time* (14 July 1961), p. 87.

21 Quoted in Robert W. Trogdon, ed., *Ernest Hemingway: A Literary Reference* (New York, 1999), p. 307.

22 A. E. Hotchner, *Papa Hemingway* (New York, 1966), p. 212; Welsh Hemingway, *How It Was*, pp. 470–72.

23 Hotchner, *Papa*, p. 206.

24 Welsh Hemingway, *How It Was*, p. 477.

25 Reynolds, *Final Years*, p. 335.

26 Ernest Hemingway, 'Neo-Thomist Poem', in *Complete Poems*, ed. Nicholas Gerogiannis (London, 1992), p. 147.

27 Hotchner, *Papa*, p. 242.
28 Welsh Hemingway, *How It Was*, pp. 489–90.
29 Hotchner, *Papa*, pp. 255–7, 265–8.
30 Untitled, *Time*, LXXVII/19 (5 May 1961), p. 36.
31 Hotchner, *Papa*, p. 228.
32 Reynolds, *Final Years*, p. 351.
33 Carlos Baker, *Ernest Hemingway: A Life Story* (New York, 1969), p. 559.
34 John F. Kennedy, Address to American Society of Newspaper Editors (20 April 1961), Papers of John F. Kennedy, Presidential Papers, President's Office Files, Speech Files, John F. Kennedy Presidential Library and Museum, Boston, MA.
35 John F. Kennedy Presidential Library and Museum, 'The Bay of Pigs', www.jfklibrary.org, accessed 4 October 2015.
36 Welsh Hemingway, *How It Was*, pp. 498–9.
37 Reynolds, *Final Years*, pp. 322–3.
38 'Rebels Invade Cuba at 3 Points; Fighting Is Brisk; U.S. Approves Aims of Revolt but Denies Giving Help', *Wall Street Journal* (18 April 1961), p. 3.
39 'Castro's Triumph', *Time*, LXXVII/19 (5 May 1961), pp. 32–5.
40 Sandra Spanier et al., eds, *The Letters of Ernest Hemingway*, vol. II: *1923–1925* (New York, 2013), p. 6; author's email correspondence with Hilary Justice (15 February 2015).
41 Author's Facebook correspondence with Susan Beegel (31 December 2014); Welsh Hemingway, *How It Was*, p. 497.
42 Welsh Hemingway, *How It Was*, p. 502.

L'Envoi

1 Ernest Hemingway, Nobel Prize acceptance speech, quoted in Robert W. Trogdon, ed., *Ernest Hemingway: A Literary Reference* (New York, 1999), p. 297.
2 Ernest Hemingway, *To Have and Have Not* (New York, 2003), p. 238.
3 'Hemingway Dead of Shotgun Wound; Wife Says He Was Cleaning Weapon', *New York Times* (3 July 1961), p. 6.
4 Valerie Hemingway, *Running with the Bulls: My Years with the Hemingways* (New York, 2005), p. 168.

5 Albert J. DeFazio III, ed., *Dear Papa, Dear Hotch: The Correspondence of Ernest Hemingway and A. E. Hotchner* (Columbia, MO, 2005), p. 11.

6 'Mrs. Hemingway Is Cautious on Publication of Manuscripts', *New York Times* (29 July 1961), p. 21.

7 Glenway Westcott, 'Hemingway's Work', Letters to the Times, *New York Times* (9 August 1961), p. 32.

8 Ernest Hemingway, *The Old Man and the Sea* (New York, 1995), p. 103.

Further Reading

Works by Hemingway

Three Stories and Ten Poems (1923)
in our time (1924)
In Our Time (1925)
The Torrents of Spring (1926)
The Sun Also Rises (1926)
Men Without Women (1927)
A Farewell to Arms (1929)
Death in the Afternoon (1932)
Winner Take Nothing (1933)
Green Hills of Africa (1935)
To Have and Have Not (1937)
The Fifth Column and the First Forty-Nine Stories (1938)
For Whom the Bell Tolls (1940)
Introduction, *Men At War: The Best War Stories of All Time* (1942)
Across the River and Into the Trees (1950)
The Old Man and the Sea (1952)
By-Line: Ernest Hemingway, ed. William White (1967)
Islands in the Stream (1970)
The Dangerous Summer (1985)
The Garden of Eden (1986)
The Complete Short Stories of Ernest Hemingway: The Finca Vigía Edition (1987)
Ernest Hemingway: Complete Poems, ed. Nicholas Gerogiannis (1992)
Under Kilimanjaro (2005)
A Moveable Feast: The Restored Edition (2009)

Letters

Baker, Carlos, ed., *Ernest Hemingway: Selected Letters* (New York, 1981)

Bruccoli, Matthew J., ed., *Fitzgerald and Hemingway: A Dangerous Friendship* (Columbia, SC, 1994)

—, ed. with the assistance of Robert W. Trogdon, *The Only Thing That Counts: The Ernest Hemingway/Maxwell Perkins Correspondence, 1925–1947* (Columbia, SC, 1996)

DeFazio III, Albert J., ed. with a Preface by A. E. Hotchner, *Dear Papa, Dear Hotch: The Correspondence of Ernest Hemingway and A. E. Hotchner* (Columbia, MO, 2005)

Sanderson, Rena, Sandra Spanier, and Robert W. Trogdon, eds, *The Letters of Ernest Hemingway*, vol. III: *1926–1929* (New York, 2015)

Spanier, Sandra, Albert J. DeFazio III and Robert W. Trogdon, eds, *The Letters of Ernest Hemingway*, vol. II: *1923–1925* (New York, 2013)

Spanier, Sandra, and Robert W. Trogdon, eds, *The Letters of Ernest Hemingway*, vol. I: *1907–1922* (New York, 2011)
    The Letters of Ernest Hemingway is an ongoing, multi-volume, comprehensive scholarly edition of all known correspondence by Ernest Hemingway. A total of at least seventeen volumes is projected. The Hemingway Letters Project is headquartered at the Pennsylvania State University and is directed by Sandra Spanier, General Editor.

Works about Hemingway

Baker, Carlos, *Ernest Hemingway: A Life Story* (New York, 1969)

Beegel, Susan F., *Hemingway's Craft of Omission: Four Manuscript Examples* (Ann Arbor, MI, 1988)

Brasch, James D., and Joseph Sigman, *Hemingway's Library: A Composite Record* (Garland, New York and London, 1981); now available online in the Ernest Hemingway Collection at the John F. Kennedy Presidential Library, www.jfklibrary.org

Broer, Lawrence R., and Gloria Holland, eds, *Hemingway and Women: Female Critics and the Female Voice* (Tuscaloosa, AL, and London, 2002)

Bruccoli, Matthew J., ed. with Judith S. Baughman, *Hemingway and the Mechanism of Fame: Statements, Public Letters, Introductions,*

Forewords, Prefaces, Blurbs, Reviews, and Endorsements (Columbia, SC, 2006)

Burwell, Rose Marie, *Hemingway: The Postwar Years and the Posthumous Novels* (Cambridge, 1996)

Donaldson, Scott, ed., *The Cambridge Companion to Ernest Hemingway* (New York, 1996)

Earle, David M., *All Man! Hemingway, 1950s Men's Magazines, and the Masculine Persona* (Kent, OH, 2009)

Hanneman, Audre, *Ernest Hemingway: A Comprehensive Bibliography* (Princeton, NJ, 1967)

—, *Supplement to Ernest Hemingway: A Comprehensive Bibliography* (Princeton, NJ, 1975)

Hemingway, Mary Welsh, *How It Was* (New York, 1976)

Justice, Hilary K., *The Bones of the Others: The Hemingway Text from the Lost Manuscripts to the Posthumous Novels* (Kent, OH, 2006)

Kennedy, J. Gerald, *Imagining Paris: Exile, Writing, and American Identity* (New Haven, CT, 1994)

Kert, Bernice, *The Hemingway Women* (New York, 1983)

Mandel, Miriam, ed., *A Companion to Hemingway's 'Death in the Afternoon'* (Rochester, NY, 2004)

—, ed., *Hemingway and Africa* (Rochester, NY, 2011)

Moddelmog, Debra A., and Suzanne del Gizzo, *Ernest Hemingway in Context* (Cambridge, 2013)

Oliver, Charles M., *Critical Companion to Ernest Hemingway: A Literary Reference to His Life and Work* (New York, 2007)

Reynolds, Michael, *Hemingway: The 1930s* (New York and London, 1997)

—, *Hemingway: The American Homecoming* (New York and London, 1992)

—, *Hemingway: The Final Years* (New York, 1999)

—, *Hemingway: The Paris Years* (New York, 1989)

—, *Hemingway's First War: The Making of 'A Farewell to Arms'* (Princeton, NJ, 1976)

—, *Hemingway's Reading 1910–1940: An Inventory* (Princeton, NJ, 1981); now available online in the Ernest Hemingway Collection at the John F. Kennedy Presidential Library, www.jfklibrary.org

—, *The Young Hemingway* (New York and London, 1986)

Smith, Paul, *A Reader's Guide to the Short Stories of Ernest Hemingway* (Boston, MA, 1989)

Trogdon, Robert W., ed., *Ernest Hemingway: A Literary Reference* (New York, 2002)
— , *The Lousy Racket: Hemingway, Scribners and the Business of Literature* (Kent, OH, 2007)
Vernon, Alex, *Hemingway's Second War: Bearing Witness to the Spanish Civil War* (Iowa City, IA, 2011)
Villard, Henry Serrano, and James Nagel, *Hemingway in Love and War: The Lost Diary of Agnes von Kurowsky, Her Letters, and Correspondence of Ernest Hemingway* (Boston, MA, 1989)
Young, Philip, *Ernest Hemingway: A Reconsideration* (University Park, PA, 1966)

Journal

del Gizzo, Suzanne, ed., *The Hemingway Review* (Moscow, ID, 1981–present)

Acknowledgements

Ernest Hemingway explained in a letter to Malcolm Cowley, 'The gen is RAF [British Royal Air Force] slang for intelligence, the hand out at the briefing. The true gen is what they know but don't tell you. The true gen very hard to obtain'.[1] The task of a biographer is to provide the gen, but here I have tried also to capture the true gen drawn from careful study of primary, secondary and archival sources during a decade-long immersion in Hemingway studies. Thus I am greatly indebted to the scholars who came before me, particularly to the work of Carlos Baker, Matthew J. Bruccoli, Rose Marie Burwell, Scott Donaldson, Bernice Kert, Miriam Mandel, Caroline Moorehead, Michael Reynolds, Paul Smith, James L. W. West III, as well as Sandra Spanier and the 'Hemteam' at the Hemingway Letters Project. A number of these influential scholars I now happily count as friends: Susan Beegel, Kirk Curnutt, Joseph Fruscione, Hilary Kovar Justice, Robert Trogdon and Lisa Tyler. My thanks go out as well to Sara Kosiba, Kevin Maier, Steve Paul, Cecil and Charlotte Ponder, and Ross Tangedal who all, at one time or another, dropped what they were doing and did the legwork for me of checking archival sources, as did my student at Hampden-Sydney College, Will Moore, who interrupted his Spring Break trip to track down a source at the Key West public library.

Thanks go especially to the colleagues who read the manuscript in draft, either in whole or in part, and offered helpful suggestions: my editor at Reaktion Books, Vivian Constantinopoulos, and her team, as well as Catherine Lowry Franssen, Hilary Kovar Justice, Lisa Tyler and Cristine Varholy. I also thank Joseph Fruscione and Jane Holland for their assistance with document preparation.

I am grateful to Ernest H. Mainland, nephew of Ernest Hemingway, and his wife Judy for their generosity and hospitality; as a guest at Windemere cottage on Walloon Lake I gained a perspective that cannot come from a library. The library is important too, however, and I owe a debt to the many librarians and archivists behind the scenes who assisted with numerous research requests, especially Maryrose Grossman, Steve Plotkin, Kristen Weischedel and Susan Wrynn at the John F. Kennedy Presidential Library; Maureen Culley, Bret Peaden and the late Gerry Randall at Hampden-Sydney College; Alex Bainbridge and Sandra Stelts at Pennsylvania State University; and staff at the Bentley Historical Library at the University of Michigan and the Knox College Library.

I am grateful to my colleagues at Hampden-Sydney College, as well as former Dean of the Faculty Robert Herdegen and Provost and Dean of the Faculty Dennis Stevens for supporting this project with summer research grants and other funding, and I thank the Hemingway Society and Ernest Hemingway Foundation for the research grant to travel to the Ernest Hemingway Collection at the John F. Kennedy Presidential Library and Museum.

Most importantly, I would like to thank my family for their encouragement, curiosity, patience and support as I worked on this book – seemingly forever. My most heartfelt thanks and love go to my husband, Steele Nowlin, and to our two children, Betty and Julian.

And, finally, I would like to acknowledge a special debt to my late friend, Michael DuBose. He loved literature unapologetically and shared that love with his students, colleagues and friends. Had he lived, he would have contributed much to the field of Hemingway studies, and so it is to him that this book is dedicated.

---

1 Carlos Baker, ed., *Ernest Hemingway: Selected Letters* (New York, 1981), p. 603.

Photo Acknowledgements

The author and the publishers wish to express their thanks to the below sources of illustrative material and/or permission to reproduce it.

From the private collection of Lucy Dos Passos Coggin: p. 55; from the private collection of David M. Earle: p. 172; Getty Images: pp. 149 (photo Archivio Cameraphoto Epoche), 162 (Earl Theisen), 166 (New York Daily News via Getty Images), 175 (Fotosearch); from the private collection of Ernest Hemingway Mainland: p. 59; John F. Kennedy Presidential Library and Museum, Boston, MA: pp. 12, 13, 24, 33 (top), 76, 94, 103, 107, 122, 132, 134, 170, 176; from the private collection of Verna Kale: pp. 33 (bottom), 180 (photograph by Kevin Maier); from the private collection of David Meeker: p. 35; from 'Ernest Hemingway letters to his family, 1901–1957', Special Collections Library, Pennsylvania State University: p. 66; REX Shutterstock: p. 8 (Everett Collection); image courtesy of Yale Collection of American Literature, Beinecke Rare Book and Manuscript Library, Yale University: p. 45.